JAN 2 2 1091

Ralph G. Brockett, *University of Tennessee, Knoxville*
EDITOR-IN-CHIEF

Alan B. Knox, *University of Wisconsin, Madison*
CONSULTING EDITOR

Serving Culturally Diverse Populations

Jovita M. Ross-Gordon
The Pennsylvania State University

Larry G. Martin
University of Wisconsin, Milwaukee

Diane Buck Briscoe
University of South Florida

EDITORS

Number 48, Winter 1990

JOSSEY-BASS INC., PUBLISHERS
San Francisco

#23019881

SERVING CULTURALLY DIVERSE POPULATIONS
Jovita M. Ross-Gordon, Larry G. Martin, Diane Buck Briscoe (eds.)
New Directions for Adult and Continuing Education, no. 48
Ralph G. Brockett, Editor-in-Chief
Alan B. Knox, Consulting Editor

Microfilm copies of issues and articles are available in 16mm and 35mm, as well as microfiche in 105mm, through University Microfilms Inc., 300 North Zeeb Road, Ann Arbor, Michigan 48106.

LC 85-644750   ISSN 0195-2242   ISBN 1-55542-802-9

NEW DIRECTIONS FOR ADULT AND CONTINUING EDUCATION is part of The Jossey-Bass Higher and Adult Education Series and is published quarterly by Jossey-Bass Inc., Publishers (publication number USPS 493-930). Second-class postage paid at San Francisco, California, and at additional mailing offices. Postmaster: Send address changes to Jossey-Bass Inc., Publishers, 350 Sansome Street, San Francisco, California 94104.

EDITORIAL CORRESPONDENCE should be sent to the Editor-in-Chief, Ralph G. Brockett, Dept. of Technological and Adult Education, University of Tennessee, 402 Claxton Addition, Knoxville, Tennessee 37996-3400.

Cover photograph by Wernher Krutein/PHOTOVAULT © 1990.

Printed on acid-free paper in the United States of America.

CONTENTS

EDITORS' NOTES

This volume, *Serving Culturally Diverse Populations*, brings together seven adult and continuing education professionals whose practice and research reflect an interest in providing effective educational programs that serve adults from culturally diverse backgrounds. In Chapter One, Jovita M. Ross-Gordon sets the stage by considering theoretical perspectives that might enhance our understanding of current patterns of participation in adult and continuing education by underrepresented racial and ethnic groups. She also provides demographic data that suggest the importance of enhancing educational opportunities for those now considered "minorities" in the United States.

In the chapters that follow, the authors provide conceptual analyses of various issues of adult education, reviews of pertinent literature, and descriptions of actual programs currently serving racial and ethnic minority adults. The particular criteria used to guide the selection of "effective" programs for description in this volume include demonstration of one or more of the following program planning or delivery characteristics.

1. Preserving cultural distinctness of groups in programming: Minorities are not expected to abandon their cultural heritage as a function of participation; all minorities are not treated alike.
2. Assessing and accommodating preferred learning styles and learning circumstances of specific minority group populations.
3. Utilizing existing social networks, whether in outreach and recruitment, program development, retention, or program follow-up.
4. Empowering learners to change their lives and their communities.
5. Preparing learners for life and career development beyond short-term occupational goals.
6. Supporting minority families in their pursuit of learning goals: Programs that are successful in this aspect might include efforts to increase minority parents' involvement in children's learning or in school effectiveness programs, or to involve family members in supporting educational reentry of adult members.
7. Reaching out to the most disenfranchised: These programs work effectively with young adult dropouts, welfare parents, drug and alcohol dependents, AIDS patients, or corrections populations.
8. Utilizing creative financing of adult learning opportunities, including financial aid counseling and brokering, private cooperation, and use of volunteers to expand program offerings.
9. Sponsoring activities that increase the level of intercultural sensitivity of staff to enhance their capacity to work with multicultural populations.

In addition to these principles of effective practice with culturally diverse adults, five broad areas of adult education practice are identified as particularly relevant to the discussion of programs effectively serving culturally diverse populations. These areas are not purported to be exhaustive of all the adult education domains in which exemplary activities exist. Rather, five areas were selected for which some literature base was available and for which program planning seems critical to the growth and development of underrepresented peoples. Within each of the selected areas, one or two chapters provide a close look at a specific educational context.

The first domain considered is that of literacy, adult basic education, and general education. Given long-standing educational inequities, the acquisition of basic literacy skills and educational competencies remains a necessary starting point of education for many persons of color. In Chapter Two, Larry G. Martin provides a close look at the factors influencing school noncompletion among minority youth and examines the role of literacy education as a form of social intervention designed to provide a point of entry or reentry into the social mainstream for the disenfranchised.

The next domain selected for inclusion is degree and certificate programs for adults. In Chapter Three, John F. Moe focuses on the involvement of minority adults in degree programs in community colleges, four-year colleges, and universities.

Workplace learning is the third adult education domain considered. In Chapter Four, Larry G. Martin and Jovita M. Ross-Gordon examine the imperative faced by the business world to provide human resource development opportunities for traditionally underrepresented peoples, as well as training for managers in their supervision of a culturally diverse work force. They outline the components of an effective training program to meet these goals.

The fourth domain considered is cultural enrichment and lifelong learning. In this category were placed programs designed to benefit individual learners with aims beyond skills development, degree completion, and job preparation or development. In Chapter Five, Ronald Podeschi reviews the historical precedent for ethnic minority populations to provide their own educational services within a culturally supportive environment. His specific case focuses on an English as a Second Language/literacy program developed by and for Hmong refugees in the Midwest. In Chapter Six, Frank E. Nardine provides a historical overview of parent education emphases, presents a theoretical framework for programs aimed at parental empowerment, and describes collaborative programs that bring together the resources of families, schools, businesses, and community agencies.

Finally, empowerment and community development serves as the fifth domain of adult education activity analyzed in this volume. In Chapter Seven, Diane Buck Briscoe reviews origins of community education, discusses changing conceptions of community, and examines the special value of community education as a catalyst for change in a "salad bowl" society. In Chapter Eight, Jorge Jeria provides a historical and conceptual overview of popular education. His discussion also examines the practice of popular education as exemplified in state and local models in a midwestern urban community and delineates several critical dimensions for understanding the distinctive features of popular education programs.

Over fifty years ago Morse Cartwright (1935, p. 155) observed, "More remains to be done in the extension of educational opportunities to Negroes than in any other field of adult and continuing education. And that much must be done, if we are to preserve the safety and integrity of our social institutions, no thoughtful student on American life will deny." With some updating to reflect contemporary ethnic labels, the message of this quote remains relevant today. As we face the challenges of developing adult and continuing education programs that are inclusive rather than exclusive in an era of increasing cultural diversity, the principles and program descriptions provided here suggest fresh approaches to old problems.

Jovita M. Ross-Gordon
Larry G. Martin
Diane Buck Briscoe
Editors

Reference

Cartwright, M. *Ten Years of Adult Education: A Report on a Decade of Progress in the American Movement.* New York: Macmillan, 1935.

Jovita M. Ross-Gordon is assistant professor of adult education at The Pennsylvania State University, University Park.

Larry G. Martin is associate professor of adult and continuing education at the University of Wisconsin, Milwaukee.

Diane Buck Briscoe is assistant professor of adult education at the University of South Florida, Tampa.

Demographic trends and recent data on participation in adult and
continuing education by minority adults suggest inequities in access.
A sociocultural perspective on participation and nonparticipation
may inform new alternatives in program development to address
these inequities.

Serving Culturally Diverse Populations: A Social Imperative for Adult and Continuing Education

Jovita M. Ross-Gordon

The progressive roots of American adult and continuing education define a concern for equitable access to adult education for all members of a democratic society (Cartwright, 1935; Locke, 1947). Yet, as a field, we must admit that participation patterns in adult and continuing education suggest differential access and utilization by groups typically referred to in our society as minorities. As groups that have been socially defined as ethnic and racial minorities increasingly move toward becoming a numerical majority in certain segments of American society (Hodgkinson, 1986), it behooves us to examine these issues in greater detail.

Background

One of the aims of this volume is to present current literature and descriptions of practice that address the phenomenon of cultural diversity, an area of critical concern for socially conscious adult educators at the close of the twentieth century. Although the proportion of the U.S. population represented by African-Americans has remained nearly 12 percent throughout the last decade, the Hispanic population has grown 30 percent since 1980, a rate five times faster than the rest of the population (Pear, 1987; U.S. Bureau of the Census, 1989). While some of this growth is due to differential birthrates, growing numbers of immigrants from Cuba, Mexico, and Central America have joined the long-standing Hispanic populations of Mexican-Americans, Puerto Ricans, and Cuban-Americans. And Laotians,

Vietnamese, and Hmong have joined Japanese-Americans, Chinese-Americans, and Koreans, increasing the diversity among Asian populations. Additionally, Blacks cannot be seen as a monolithic group, since African and West Indian immigrants and Afro-Hispanics bring their own cultural backgrounds and educational needs, distinct from those of African-Americans who have lived in this country for many generations. In the chapters that follow, we attempt to share a vision for effectively serving culturally diverse populations in U.S. adult education programs. We have chosen to focus primarily on several racial and ethnic minorities that can be viewed as indigenous to the United States, given their long-standing presence—Native Americans, African-Americans, and Hispanic Americans (of Mexican and Puerto Rican ancestry). These groups are distinguished by the means through which they historically came to be a part of the cultural fabric of the United States: the slave trade and geographic intrusions (Deloria, 1981). In this regard they are unlike the groups who immigrated voluntarily to the United States. Due to both structural social factors and efforts to preserve cultural identity, their assimilation into the dominant culture has in many ways been less than complete. This context necessitates culturally sensitive educational programming. The educational disadvantage experienced historically by these groups suggests that special attention must be given to facilitating their inclusion in adult education programs. This may in some cases require programmatic efforts not necessary with native-born Whites and immigrant populations who may more actively seek existing adult education opportunities.

Before we cast our attention to exemplary adult and continuing education efforts, it is important that we first briefly review the general status of affairs of adult education service to minority group adults. Subsequently, we examine alternative explanations for their disproportionately low participation rates in formal adult education programs.

Participation Levels

The landmark adult education participation study by Johnstone and Rivera (1965) reported 9 percent of those participating in adult education were Black, compared to 12 percent of their total sample. Whites comprised 90 percent of the adult education participants, although they only made up 88 percent of the sample. Figures were not given for any other racial or ethnic category. The most recent data from the National Center for Education Statistics indicate that 8.1 percent of Blacks, 8.2 percent of Hispanics, and 14.5 percent of Whites participated in adult education in 1984 (Snyder, 1988). A study of trends in adult education from 1969 to 1984 (Hill, 1987) revealed that Blacks made up 6 percent of adult education participants in 1984, compared to 7 percent in 1969. During the same time period, Blacks increased as a segment of the population seventeen years of age and over from 10 percent to 11 percent (Hill, 1987, p. 3). Whites remained a steady 92 percent of the adult education participant group, while dropping in representation among the adult population from 89 percent to 86 percent. Trends could not be observed for Hispanics since they did not appear as a separate category in 1969. Generally, the lack of statistics on adult education participation that report both learners' race or ethnicity and type of program make it difficult to comment on the success of adult educators in reaching the various culturally and ethnically defined groups of learners within distinct segments of adult and continuing education.

A number of demographic factors may be linked to the disproportionately low participation rates of African-Americans and Hispanics in adult education programs. Overrepresented as participants in adult education are Whites, persons with a college education, persons living in the western United States, persons with above-median incomes, and persons working in executive, professional, or technical occupations (Hill, 1987, p. 2). Darkenwald and Merriam (1982) have suggested that education is more important than race in predicting participation, since well-educated Blacks participate at similar levels to Whites. High school completion seems to be a critical marker in predicting future adult education participation. With high school completion rates for Hispanics and Blacks in 1986 at 58.9 percent and 72 percent, respectively, compared to a completion rate for Whites at 80.8 percent (U.S. Bureau of the Census, 1989, p. 146), part of the discrepancy in participation levels appears to be explained by differences in educational attainment.

To the extent that participation in adult education also increases with income level (U.S. Bureau of the Census, 1989), income differences between Whites and non-Whites are also likely to be related to different participation rates. Williams (1987) notes that 29 percent of Black working couples earned incomes below the poverty level in 1984, while only 17 percent of White working couples earned similar incomes. Economic problems are especially acute for minority female-headed households. Black female-headed households reported a median income in 1984 of $8,648, just 57 percent of the median income for White female-headed households (Williams, 1987); Hispanic women in 1983 earned a median income of $11,874, compared to white women at $14,479 (Hernandez, 1987). If we simply assume that minorities will eventually participate in adult and continuing education at equitable levels once they have caught up in prior education and income, we ignore the social inequalities that perpetuate such discrepancies.

The ethos of adult education in years past placed a great value on adult education as a means of improving social conditions (Apps, 1989; Griffith, 1989; Stubblefield and Keane, 1989). Observers of trends in adult education today are likely to perceive a greater preoccupation with market-driven domains of adult education like human resource development and continuing professional education. Yet, recent reports on labor force participation and economic development suggest the social improvement function of adult education may be of critical importance in coming years, even in relationship to the current emphasis on workplace learning. The report "The Forgotten Half: Non-College Youth in America" documents the findings of a nineteen-member two-year panel called the Commission on Work, Family, and Citizenship, funded by the William T. Grant Foundation (1988; see also Viadero, 1988). This report raises striking issues regarding the economic fate of all young adults seeking career entry in contemporary times without a college degree and urges educational intervention specifically targeted to this population. The report documents an increasing number of young adults who have slipped below the poverty level despite holding a high school diploma—and the economic picture is more severe for Black and Hispanic males between twenty and twenty-five years of age in this educational category than it is for Whites. At the same time, participation rates in higher education by minorities have held steady or increased during the last decade for Asians and Hispanics, while declining for Native Americans and African-Americans (Wilson and Carter, 1988, p. 23).

Analysts looking at the changing face of the American workplace have emphasized the declining presence of the White male as increasing proportions of workers are female, native-born minorities, or immigrants (Ehrlich and Garland, 1988; National Alliance of Business, 1986; Nussbaum, 1988). Without a significant increase in their college participation rates or adult education experiences to provide further education, many from this growing minority segment of the work force will find themselves relegated to low-level service occupations. The disappearance of the industrial economy and its replacement by a technology-based information economy may have a major impact on the economic status of minority workers. While African-Americans and Hispanics are proportionately represented or over-represented in a number of rapidly growing occupational areas such as cooks, guards, health aids, and computer operators, they are underrepresented in the more financially lucrative and highly trained growth occupations such as managers and executives, registered nurses, computer systems analysts, computer programmers, and electronics engineers (U.S. Bureau of the Census, 1989, pp. 387, 391).

The employment patterns of minorities may also influence participation in adult education through variables other than income alone. Hill (1987) notes that among the major trends in adult education between 1969 and 1984 were changes in the providers and financing of adult education. Nonschool providers of adult education became more important, increasing their share from 37 percent to 46 percent (1987, pp. 12-13). Counted for the first time as a provider of adult education in 1972, business and industry provided nearly as many courses to adults in 1984 (6,850,000) as four-year colleges and universities (6,900,000) (1987, pp. 11, 13). Similarly, vocational, trade, and business schools offered a growing number of adult education courses, up from 1,800,000 in 1969 to 4,000,000 in 1964. Meanwhile, elementary and secondary schools provided fewer adult education courses in 1984 than in 1969. This report documents that although women accounted for much of the increase in employment-related adult education (up from one-half to two-thirds of all adult education courses), employers provided a higher proportion of the job-related adult education taken by men (44 percent) than by women (38 percent) in 1984. Although the report by Hill does not address access of minorities to employer-provided or employer-supported education, another recent study did examine these patterns. Based on analysis of data collected in the triennial survey of adult education between 1969 and 1981, Zemsky, Tierney, Berg, and Scach-Marquez, 1983, p. 8) concluded, regarding employer-provided education, that "even when education and age were taken into account, non-whites, particularly those with minimal levels of schooling, [received] significantly less training than similarly schooled whites in the same age group." On a more encouraging note, non-Whites were more likely than Whites to have participated in employer-sponsored education and training, with the exception of a downturn in minority participation in 1978 (1983, pp. 30–31). The authors noted that employer-sponsored education more likely occurs in two-year and four-year colleges and universities and observed with curiosity a similar downturn in minority participation in higher education during 1978. It would obviously be of value to determine whether the observed patterns regarding minority participation in employer-provided and employer-sponsored education have held steady during the decade of the 1980s.

Perspectives on Low Participation Levels by Minorities

A number of explanations can be posed about why adults from culturally diverse backgrounds seem to be disinclined to participate in traditional adult education programs. Both psychosocial and sociological theories seem to offer insight. To the extent that these models include socioeconomic class as an important variable, rather than race or ethnicity, it is important to note that adults from the minority groups emphasized in this volume can be found across the socioeconomic strata. Significant evidence suggests, however, that they are disproportionately located in the lower socioeconomic strata, using common criteria of income, educational level, and occupational status.

Psychosocial Models of Motivation for Participation. Rubenson's Expectancy-Valence paradigm (cited in Cross, 1981) builds on the work of Lewin (1951) and others who explain human behavior in terms of interaction between individual and environment. Motivation to participate is said to result from a combination of personal and environmental factors that influences two critical components, expectancy and valence. Rubenson conceptualizes expectancy in terms of two dimensions. First, there must be an expectation of personal success in the educational activity. Second, there must be an expectation that being successful in the learning activity will have positive consequences. Valence, the second component, is interrelated with the second dimension of expectancy. For any possible act of participation, the individual anticipates possible outcomes, some of which may be negative, others of which may be positive. Valence is conceptualized as the algebraic sum of the positive and negative consequences. For instance, anticipated loss of social acceptance or immediate income benefits may outweigh the benefits of earning a general equivalency diploma for some individuals. The combined force of valence and expectancy is said to determine the likelihood of participation. Following this model, Joseph, for example, whose prior educational experiences lead him to doubt that he will succeed in the given educational opportunity, would be predicted to decline participation in a program of study because of low expectation. Lourdes may view herself as a successful learner who would succeed if she tried and may find the given educational program desirable. However, anticipated barriers such as lack of spousal support and difficulties finding child care may combine with her observations of the difficulty a friend has had in finding employment in the area of her associate degree. In the end, she would probably not choose to participate.

The Cross (1981) Chain-of-Response model provides another conceptualization of motivation to participate in adult education. According to this model, participation is not a single act but rather a chain of responses, each based on evaluation of the position of the individual in his or her environment. The individual considering participation in an educational activity begins with a self-evaluation. This self-evaluation is influenced by the individual's attitudes toward education, which arise both directly from the learner's own past experience and indirectly from attitudes and experiences of friends and "significant others." Negative attitudes due to previous educational failure or attitudes of the reference group may prevent further consideration of the learning opportunity at that point. If the learner is positively motivated to that point, Cross hypothesizes that valence (the importance of the goals to the learner) and expectancy (a subjective judgment that pursuit of the goals will lead to desired outcomes) then come into play. If a minority adult doubts that participating in the educational experience will lead to any tangible changes in his or her life situation, motivation to participate may be reduced.

Life transitions may also play a role in the motivational process, often creating a need for new learning related to work, family, or some other domain of life that increases the importance of the learning goal, or the valence. The minority mother who has recently become a single parent is likely to experience a "teachable moment" when she realizes that further education might enable her to support her family more effectively. Finally, if the learner has maintained an interest in participation to this point, institutional or situational barriers and opportunities increase or decrease the chance of participation. The learner may be motivated by flexible class hours but discouraged by learner fees and difficulty finding child care. Accessible and accurate information is also essential for a positive choice at this stage, since without it learners may be unaware either of the educational opportunity itself or of needed support services that may be available, such as financial aid or a child-care cooperative.

The adult educator would seem to have at least partial control over availability of information and reduction of barriers to participation. The educator interested in recruiting underrepresented adults must make special efforts to determine the most effective means of promoting programs in their communities. Location of programs can be made convenient, fees can be kept to a minimum, and scheduling of programs and services can be planned with the needs of adults in mind. Yet, Cross (1981) notes that removal of external barriers alone has done little to increase participation by Blacks. She suggests that creation of new opportunities is not enough to overcome negative forces built up at earlier points in the motivation model. Note that the models presented in this volume typically go beyond the simple removal of barriers.

Sociological Theories of Education. Some have discussed the negative forces at points A (self-evaluation), B (attitudes about education), and C (importance of goals and expectation that participation will meet goals) primarily in psychological terms, focusing on low self-esteem and negative attitudes of the referent group as barriers to participation. Keddie (1980) notes that the concept of disadvantage in adult education often reflects a concern with helping the supposedly different adult, but it neglects to challenge the modes by which education controls differential access to knowledge and power. An examination of the past schooling experiences of many racially and ethnically defined minority adults can provide an alternative interpretation of the reasons for their withdrawal from formal education. Fine (1985) suggests that societal inequities as well as institutional barriers contribute to the "purging" of minority students from schools, whether by coercion or by choice. High school noncompletion rates for Hispanics, ranging from 33 percent to as high as 88 percent of a cohort (National Center for Education Statistics, 1982; Orum, 1984; Valverde, 1987), can hardly be attributed to different ability levels. Even if poor self-esteem and motivation are posed as explanations, one must consider what within the schooling experience contributes to such psychological states.

Educational sociologists subscribing to a social reproduction theory of education would explain this phenomenon in terms of economic, cultural, or hegemonic reproduction, focusing, respectively, on the function of the school in reproducing labor stratification, legitimizing selected knowledge, values, and language, or preserving ideological imperatives of the state (Giroux, 1983). In this theoretical tradition, teachers and students are portrayed as often-unwitting actors, teaching and learning a hidden curriculum that preserves the status quo (Apple, 1979).

Resistance theory (Giroux, 1983) may offer a more plausible alternative interpretation of nonparticipation than does social reproduction theory, since while acknowledging the hegemonic forces, resistance theory gives more credit to the agency of teachers and learners. Learners or teachers may passively or aggressively resist the perceived inequities of society as transmitted through school culture. Dropout from the formal educational system can be interpreted in this light as active resistance to co-optation by a system that does not value or nurture the full range of the learner's abilities and interests. Following along these lines, Ogbu (1987, p. 263) describes a collective process of cultural inversion through which members of a minority group may reject "certain forms of behavior, certain events, symbols, and meanings as not appropriate to them because they are characteristics of members of another population (e.g., White Americans); at the same time, however, they claim other forms of behavior, other events, symbols, and meanings as appropriate for them because these are not characteristics of the members of the other population. Thus what is appropriate or even legitimate behavior for the in-group members is defined in opposition to the practices and preferences of the members of an outgroup." He notes that such inversion is practiced selectively, rather than occurring in all areas of culture, but contends that such processes often affect school performance. As an example he notes that African-Americans have long expressed high educational aspirations and have engaged in a collective struggle for equal access to good schooling. Yet, he suggests factors such as disillusionment arising from perceived job ceilings, folk theories of success and failure, conflicts with and distrust of the schools, and an oppositional cultural frame of reference "make it difficult for Blacks and similar minorities to learn and demonstrate persevering academic attitudes and efforts required for success in school" (Ogbu, 1987, p. 269).

One might ask, what does resistance to compulsory schooling have to do with adult education participation? Are we not, after all, providing forms of education that acknowledge and respond to the felt needs of the learners? Can't the learner who rejected or felt rejected by the basic education system appreciate the opportunity to gain a second chance through the adult education system?

Learner perceptions that associate all formal education with earlier learning experiences often prevent a try-it-and-see approach. Even when an attempt is made, what is found may not be radically different in content of process from earlier, negative education experiences. Adult education programs may be no more likely than kindergarten-to-twelfth-grade and higher education programs to acknowledge the learning styles of minority learners and may present content that falls short of recognizing the real-life cultural perspectives and learning needs of racial and ethnic minority participants. Keddie (1980) maintains that adult education is more similar than dissimilar to the rest of education in its forms of cultural reproduction. Like the two Canadian Indian women whose departure from an adult basic education program inspired his research, the educational resisters examined through literature analysis by Quigley (1990) were resisting normative values and cultural systems. To counter such resistance, Quigley (1990, p. 113) calls for the development of alternate programs "grounded in acceptable/relevant values and cultural systems by seeking learning possibilities with resisters and their significant others."

Self-Directed and Nonformal Learning. A focus on low levels of participation by minority adults in traditional formal adult education, as we have thus far adopted here, provides a partial misrepresentation of reality. This picture ignores the often self-designed adult learning actively pursued within community-based adult education organizations (Hamilton and Cunningham, 1989; Upton, 1984; Roberts, 1982), churches (Deck, 1986; Chatham and Redbird-Selam, 1972; Lloyd, 1976), and voluntary organizations (Baba, Abonyi, and Hawk, 1979; Hoffman, 1983; Muraskin, 1976; Perilla and Orum, 1984). Although this volume does not focus on such efforts in detail, the success of such endeavors suggests that the design of programs that address the social, economic, and cultural values of minority communities can indeed increase levels of participation. Thus, one of the aims of this volume is to examine adult education programs that have succeeded in incorporating many of the features found in such community-based, nonformal adult education programs.

Conclusion

Demographic changes provide compelling reasons for increasing concern about the continuing underrepresentation of ethnic and racial minorities in adult education programs. Theoretical explanations for decreased levels of participation are likely to be enhanced by greater attention to the social and cultural forces that impinge on the individual's likeliness to be motivated toward participation in formal adult education programs. Likewise, more effective models of adult education practice in minority communities are likely to result from an improved understanding of the sociocultural contexts of the intended learners.

References

Apple, M. *Ideology and Curriculum.* Boston: Routledge & Kegan Paul, 1979.
Apps, J. "What Should the Future Focus Be for Adult and Continuing Education?" In B. A. Quigley (ed.), *Fulfilling the Promise of Adult and Continuing Education.*

New Directions for Continuing Education, no. 44. San Francisco: Jossey-Bass, 1989.

Baba, M. L., Abonyi, M. H., and Hawk, M. *Mexicans of Detroit.* Peopling of Michigan Series. Detroit, Mich.: Wayne State University, Center for Urban Studies, 1979. (ED 224 650)

Cartwright, M. *Ten Years of Adult Education: A Report on a Decade of Progress in the American Movement.* New York: Macmillan, 1935.

Chatham, R. L., and Redbird-Selam, H. M. (eds.). *Indian Adult Education and the Voluntary Sector.* Proceedings of a conference sponsored by Church Women United. Monmouth: Oregon College of Education, 1972. (ED 072 333)

Cross, K. P. *Adults as Learners: Increasing Participation and Facilitating Learning.* San Francisco: Jossey-Bass, 1981.

Darkenwald, G. G., and Merriam, S. B. *Adult Education: Foundations of Practice.* New York: Harper & Row, 1982.

Deck, A. F. "Hispanic Ministry Comes of Age." *America,* 1986, *154* (18), 400–402.

Deloria, V. "Identity and Culture." *Daedalus,* 1981, *110* (2), 13–28.

Ehrlich, I. F., and Garland, S. B. "For American Business, a New World of Workers." *Business Week,* Sept. 19, 1988, pp. 112–120.

Fine, M. "Dropping Out of High School: An Inside Look." *Social Policy,* 1985, *16* (2), 43–50.

Giroux, H. "Theories of Reproduction and Resistance in the New Sociology of Education: A Critical Analysis." *Harvard Educational Review,* 1983, *53* (3), 257–293.

Griffith, W. S. "Has Adult and Continuing Education Fulfilled Its Early Promise?" In B. A. Quigley (ed.), *Fulfilling the Promise of Adult and Continuing Education.* New Directions for Continuing Education, no. 44. San Francisco: Jossey-Bass, 1989.

Hamilton, E., and Cunningham, P. "Community-Based Adult Education." In S. B. Merriam and P. M. Cunningham (eds.), *Handbook of Adult and Continuing Education.* San Francisco: Jossey-Bass, 1989.

Hernandez, A. "Hispanic Women." In L. Tarr-Whelan and L. C. Isensee (eds.), *The Women's Economic Justice Agenda: Ideas for the States.* Washington, D.C.: National Center for Policy Alternatives, 1987.

Hill, S. *Trends in Adult Education, 1969–1984.* Washington, D.C.: National Center for Education Statistics, 1987. (ED 282 054)

Hodgkinson, H. L. *Guess Who's Coming to Work.* Occasional Papers, no. 116. Columbus: Ohio State University, National Center for Research in Vocational Education, 1986. (ED 269 646)

Hoffman, S. *In Recognition of Culture: A Resource Guide for Adult Educators About Women of Color.* Tallahassee: Florida State Department of Education, 1983. (ED 236 419)

Johnstone, J., and Rivera, A. *Volunteers for Learning.* Hawthorne, N.Y.: Aldine, 1965.

Keddie, N. "Adult Education: An Ideology of Individualism." In J. Thompson (ed.), *Adult Education for a Change.* London: Hutchison, 1980.

Lewin, K. *Field Theory in Social Science: Related Theoretical Papers.* D. Cartwright (ed.). New York: Harper & Row, 1951.

Lloyd, G. "A Quarter Century of the Black Experience with the Church, 1950–1974." *Negro Educational Review,* 1976, *27* (1), 34–45.

Locke, A. "Education for Adulthood." *Adult Education Journal,* 1947, *6,* 104–111.

Muraskin, W. "The Hidden Role of Fraternal Organizations in the Education of Black Adults: Prince Hall Freemasonry as a Case Study." *Adult Education,* 1976, *26* (4), 235–252.

National Alliance of Business. *Employment Policies: Looking to the Year 2000.* Washington, D.C.: National Alliance of Business, 1986.

National Center for Education Statistics. *Digest of Education Statistics.* Office of

Educational Research and Improvement and the National Center for Education Statistics. Washington, D.C.: Government Printing Office, 1982.

Nussbaum, B. "Needed: Human Capital." *Business Week*, Sept. 19, 1988, pp. 100-103.

Ogbu, J. U. "Variability in Minority Responses to Schooling: Nonimmigrants Versus Immigrants." In G. Spindler and L. Spindler (eds.), *Interpretive Ethnography of Education: At Home and Abroad*. Hillsdale, N.J.: Erlbaum, 1987.

Orum, L. S. *Hispanic Dropouts: Community Responses*. Washington, D.C.: Office of Research, Advocacy, and Legislation and National Council of La Raza, 1984.

Pear, R. "Hispanic Population Growing Five Times as Fast as Rest of U.S." *New York Times*, Sept. 11, 1987, p. A1.

Perilla, A., and Orum, L. *Working Together: A Guide to Community-Based Educational Resources and Programs*. (2nd ed.) Washington, D.C.: National Council of La Raza, 1984. (ED 253 606)

Quigley, B. A. "Hidden Logic: Reproduction and Resistance in Adult Literacy and Adult Basic Education." *Adult Education Quarterly*, 1990, 40 (2), 103-115.

Roberts, H. *Culture and Adult Education: A Study of Alberta and Quebec*. Edmonton, Canada: University of Alberta Press, 1982.

Snyder, T. *Digest of Education Statistics*. Office of Educational Research and Improvement and the National Center for Education Statistics. Washington, D.C.: Government Printing Office, 1988.

Stubblefield, H., and Keane, P. "The History of Adult and Continuing Education." In S. B. Merriam and P. M. Cunningham (eds.), *Handbook of Adult and Continuing Education*. San Francisco: Jossey-Bass, 1989.

U.S. Bureau of the Census, Department of Commerce. *Statistical Abstracts of the United States*. Washington, D.C.: Government Printing Office, 1989.

Upton, J. N. "Applied Black Studies: Adult Education in the Black Community—A Case Study." *Journal of Negro Education*, 1984, 54, 322-333.

Valverde, S. A. "A Comparative Study of Hispanic High School Dropouts and Graduates." *Education and Urban Society*, 1987, 19 (3), 320-329.

Viadero, P. "Economic Prospects Said Bleak for the 'Forgotten Half.' " *Education Week*, Jan. 27, 1988, p. 1.

William T. Grant Foundation. *The Forgotten Half: Non-College Youth in America*. Washington, D.C.: William T. Grant Foundation Commission on Work, Family, and Citizenship, 1988.

Williams, L. F. "Black Women." In L. Tarr-Whelan and L. C. Isensee (eds.), *The Women's Economic Justice Agenda: Ideas for the States*. Washington, D.C.: National Center for Policy Alternatives, 1987.

Wilson, R., and Carter, D. *Minorities in Higher Education. 7th Annual Status Report*. Washington, D.C.: American Council on Education, 1988.

Zemsky, R., Tierney, M., Berg, I., and Scach-Marquez, J. *Training's Benchmarks. A Statistical Sketch of Employer-Provided Training and Education, 1969–1981. Task 1 Report: The Impact of Public Policy on Education and Training in the Private Sector*. Washington, D.C.: National Institute of Education, 1983. (ED 265 379)

Jovita M. Ross-Gordon is assistant professor of adult education at The Pennsylvania State University, University Park. She has published extensively on adult learning and instruction as related to underrepresented populations of adult learners, including women, minorities, and individuals with learning disabilities.

By discovering the cultural differences that exist among adult minority students, literacy practitioners can more effectively address the learning needs of involuntary minorities.

Facilitating Cultural Diversity in Adult Literacy Programs

Larry G. Martin

Over the past two decades, minorities have comprised a significant proportion of the participants in adult literacy programs. Many of them bring to the program unique cultural perspectives that inform their attitudes, values, and educational expectations. Because the cultural perspectives and levels of educational success vary among minorities, their perspectives can be problematic for those adult literacy programs that assume all minorities represent one monolithic population.

This chapter explores the issue of facilitating cultural diversity in adult literacy programs. It is organized into four sections: a cultural model of minorities, historical context of adult literacy among minorities, culturally derived barriers to participation and completion, and a model adult literacy program.

A Cultural Model of Minorities

The cultural model of minorities proposed by Ogbu (1990) suggests that the experiences and perceptions of U.S. minorities are shaped by the initial terms of their incorporation into American society, and their subsequent treatment by White Americans. This paradigm is composed of three educationally relevant groups: autonomous minorities, immigrant (or voluntary) minorities, and castelike (or involuntary minorities). Both voluntary and involuntary minorities face discrimination in various spheres of American life, such as employment (through job ceilings where they are relegated to menial jobs and low wages), social and geographical segregation, and inferior and segregated schools. However, through a comparative analysis

NEW DIRECTIONS FOR ADULT AND CONTINUING EDUCATION, no. 48, Winter 1990 ©Jossey-Bass Inc., Publishers of the historical, structural, and psychological factors influencing school-adjustment problems of voluntary and involuntary minorities, Ogbu (1990) demonstrates why the latter are plagued by persistently poor academic performance while the former are not.

Autonomous Minorities. While autonomous minorities, such as Jews and Mormons, may be victims of prejudice, the social stratification that plagues other minorities does not define their socioeconomic status (Ogbu, 1990). By employing a cultural frame of reference that encourages success, they deflect the prejudicial effects of their minority status.

Voluntary Minorities. Voluntary minorities, such as the Chinese, Central and South American Latinos, Cubans, and Koreans, have chosen to move to the United States in efforts to obtain either economic well-being or greater political freedom (Ogbu, 1990). Therefore, they have as their reference group not White Americans or other minorities but rather the peers in their former homelands. They tend to retain a keen sense of who they were before they emigrated and thereby perceive their social identities as different from, not opposed to, the identity of White Americans. The cultural backgrounds and collective social identities of voluntary minorities allow them to interpret their low socioeconomic status and the prejudice and discrimination they experience as temporary. They tend to perceive schooling, knowledge, and individual effort as the primary means of economic advancement and thereby pursue English as a Second Language and adult literacy programs with the strong expectation of adapting to and succeeding in mainstream American culture.

Involuntary Minorities. Involuntary minorities, such as American Indians, African-Americans, Puerto Ricans, Mexican-Americans, and native Hawaiians, are people who were initially brought into the United States via slavery, conquest, or colonization (Ogbu, 1990). Collectively, they resent the loss of their former freedom and interpret the economic, social, and political barriers against them not as temporary but rather as undeserved oppression. Because they compare their situation with that of their White American peers, they recognize that they belong to subordinate and disparaged minority groups. The prejudice they experience seems permanent and institutionalized.

Involuntary minorities perceive their social identity not as different from but as opposed to the social identity of White Americans. Additionally, their respective histories of struggle with intractable discrimination have continuously confirmed the derailment of their attempts to advance socioeconomically along the routes accessible to White Americans (Ogbu, 1990). Because educational institutions are perceived as embodiments of the society that oppresses them, involuntary minorities tend to view educational programs ambivalently. They thereby represent the most difficult group to recruit and retain in adult literacy programs.

The Historical Context of Adult Literacy
Among Minorities

Educational Attainment. During the past several decades the level of educational attainment among adult minorities in the United States has increased exponentially. From 1940 to 1986 the median educational attainment for minority adults aged twenty-five and over increased 7.1 grade levels: from 5.7 to 12.8 (National Center for Education Statistics, 1988). Whites in 1940 had a median of 8.7 grade levels. By 1986 their level of attainment had increased 4.2 years, to a median of 12.9 grade levels. During this same period, the median educational attainment for all adults increased 4.8 grade levels, from 8.1 to 12.9.

During the past decade, minorities have also begun to increase their rate of acquiring high school diplomas and equivalency certificates. This increase is evident in the declining percentages of youthful school non-completers for different racial groups (National Center for Education Statistics, 1988). From 1970 to 1986 the percentage of African-Americans, fourteen to thirty-four years of age, without a high school diploma declined 14.5 percent, from 30 percent to 15.5 percent. During this same period, the percentage of White noncompleters declined 3.9 percent, from 15.2 percent to 11.3 percent. Also, in eleven years, the percentage of Hispanic noncompleters declined a modest .8 percent, from 33 percent in 1975 to 32.2 percent in 1986.

The increasing educational attainment of youthful minorities, however, has not made a significant impact on the proportion of adult minorities in the general population who did not complete high school. The proportion of minority noncompleters significantly trails that of Whites. In 1986, 35.6 percent of African-Americans and 49.4 percent of Hispanics (ages eighteen and over) had not completed high school, as compared to only 23.2 percent of Whites (National Center for Education Statistics, 1988). These observations notwithstanding, Whites still constitute the largest population of school noncompleters. In 1986, Whites represented 73.7 percent of noncompleters, compared to 14.2 percent of African-Americans, and 12.1 percent of Hispanics.

Functional Literacy. Minorities have demonstrated impressive gains in educational attainment and reduced rates of school noncompletion. However, their levels of functional literacy could be their educational "Achilles' heel." Although a spate of functional literacy studies have found a disparity between the functional skills of minorities and whites, a recent national study illustrated the seriousness of the gap. Defining literacy as "using printed and written information in society, to achieve one's goals, and to develop one's knowledge and potential" (p. 3), Kirsch and Jungeblut (1986) assessed the prose comprehension, document literacy, quantitative literacy, and reading knowledge and skills of persons twenty-one to twenty-five years of age (excluding persons not living in households and those unable to speak English).

The results indicated that at Level 3 (the highest level), the functional ability of minorities significantly trailed that of Whites. Only 12 percent of Hispanics and 3.1 percent of African-Americans scored at Level 3 in prose comprehension, whereas 24.9 percent of Whites scored in this range. In terms of document literacy, 6.7 percent of Hispanics and 2.5 percent of African-Americans scored at Level 3, compared to 24 percent of Whites. Also, 11.3 percent of Hispanics and 2.4 percent of African-Americans scored at Level 3 for quantitative literacy, as opposed to 27.2 percent of Whites. In reading, Hispanics and African-Americans scored, respectively, 18.4 and 41 points below the average score of 305, while Whites scored 8.8 points above the average. (The data on Hispanic functional literacy should be interpreted with caution because the study excluded non-English-speaking subjects.)

Participation in Adult Literacy Programs. Minorities have a long history of involvement in federally funded, state-sponsored adult literacy programs. During the years between 1977–1978 and 1988–1989, the percentage of minorities enrolled in adult literacy programs increased from 54.8 percent to 60.8 percent (Pugsley, 1987; personal communication with Ronald Pugsley, February 1990). There was also a sharp difference in the rate of increase in participation experienced by different ethnic groups. For example, from 1977–1978 to 1985–1986 the rate of participation for Asians and Hispanics increased an average of 137.4 percent (which likely reflects immigration patterns), compared to an average increase of 21.5 percent for African-Americans and Native Americans, and an increase of 45.7 percent for Whites.

Table 1 presents the educational attainment levels and rates of participation in adult literacy programs achieved by the various ethnic groups. As these data document for the period 1985–1986, in adult basic education classes (Level 1) the percentage of Hispanics was double the rate of African-Americans and five times the rate of Whites. In adult secondary education classes (Level 2) Hispanics were significantly more likely to be enrolled than African-Americans and were twice as likely to be enrolled as Whites.

My search of the literature yielded no data on the rate of minority completion of literacy programs. However, data from a nationally representative sample of spring 1980 examinees for the general equivalency diploma (GED) suggest that minorities were less likely than Whites to take the GED tests. As Malizio and Whitney (1981) reported, 79 percent of the sample of GED examinees were White, about 18 percent were African-American, and 3 percent were other races. Additionally, Kirsch and Jungeblut (1986) identified a population of young adults who did not complete twelfth grade and who studied for the GED. Of this population, African-Americans (55.7 percent) were most likely to study for the tests compared

Table 1. Minority Participation in Adult Literacy Programs

Ethnic Group	Target Population Level 1[a] 1986	ABE Participants Level 1[b] 1985–86	Rate (%)	Target Population Level 2[a] 1986	ASE Participants Level 2[b] 1985–86	Rate (%)	Average Rate (%)
African-American	3,054	314	10.3	3,689	181	4.9	7.34
Hispanic	3,690	806	21.8	2,039	142	7.0	16.55
White	16,772	648	3.9	18,108	479	2.7	3.23
Total	23,516	1,768	7.5	23,836	802	3.4	5.42

Note: The U.S. Census does not include American Indians and Asians as distinct populations. Consequently, no comparisons could be made regarding the rates of participation for these ethnic groups. Level 1 attainment is eight years or less of formal education. Level 2 attainment is one to three years of high school. Population and participant figures are in thousands. ABE = adult basic education classes, ASE = adult secondary education classes.

[a] Source: National Center for Education Statistics, 1988.

[b] Source: Pugsley, 1987.

to Whites (45.8 percent) and Hispanics (43.3 percent). In contrast, they found that of those who studied for the tests, African-Americans (22.5 percent) were least likely to receive the GED compared to Whites (44.1 percent) and Hispanics (44.9 percent).

In summary, the historical context of adult literacy among minorities suggests that the mantle of educational opportunity falls unevenly on minority groups. In the absence of specific research studies designed to investigate the different levels of educational success experienced by minorities, the above data suggest a hypothesis that voluntary minorities (such as Asians and immigrant Hispanics) experience more success in adult literacy than involuntary minorities (such as African-Americans and American Indians). Proportionately, they tend to be overrepresented among participants in adult literacy programs and recipients of GED certificates. Involuntary minorities consistently increased their levels of educational attainment (over a period of forty-six years) and proportionately were overrepresented among participants in literacy programs when compared to White Americans. However, the low levels of functional literacy and GED examination and completion experienced by involuntary minorities (particularly young African-Americans) suggest that they face monumental obstacles in their quest for access to socioeconomic mobility through culturally sensitive educational environments.

Culturally Derived Barriers to Participation and Completion

If we accept Ogbu's (1990) hypothesis that involuntary minorities resist cultural assimilation by practicing a system of *cultural inversion,* that is, forms of behavior, events, symbols, and meanings that inform a social identity opposed to the social identity of White Americans, then how can adult literacy programs facilitate the learning needs of these students? One approach to this question is to consider the barriers to participation that are unique to involuntary minorities. Although they share many of the barriers (such as low self-confidence, social disapproval, situational barriers, negative attitudes toward classes, and low personal priority [Hayes and Darkenwald, 1988]) that affect other economically disadvantaged populations, involuntary minorities differ in the extent of deprivation suffered and the meaning perspectives that inform the reasons for these observed barriers. The culturally derived barriers to participation by involuntary minorities tend to reside in the social-structural forces that shape their environments, the disjunctions between primary/secondary and nondominant/dominant discourses, and culturally insensitive adult literacy programs.

Social-Structural Forces. The social-structural forces that shape the social context of involuntary minorities largely reflect the realities of a brutal capitalist economy that is profit-driven and relentless in its search for new markets. Equally a culprit is our representative (as opposed to participatory) democracy that operates more on wealth and socioeconomic status than on the perspectives of each individual citizen. During the decade of the 1980s, these forces converged to create a social context of seemingly insurmountable barriers to the participation of involuntary minorities in adult literacy programs.

The theory of human capital and skills deficit (Wacquant and Wilson, 1989), which characterizes the experiences of inner-city minorities, argues that during the 1970s and 1980s major U.S. cities experienced social-structural transformation. As they went from centers of production and distribution of goods to centers of administration, finance, and information exchange, large numbers of minorities lost their jobs. Their blue-collar jobs were replaced in part by knowledge-intensive white-collar jobs that required educational credentials at or above the level of a high school diploma. Consequently, they lacked the educational credentials to be competitive in the new economy. In the nation's largest inner cities, the loss of jobs and other structural changes led to a *hyperghettoization* (that is, the disorganization of the ghettos) of lower-class minority communities and a rising, but geographically and socially disconnected, underclass population. Hyperghettoization has resulted in a variety of social ills that have long been associated with segregated poverty: violent crime, illicit drugs, housing deterioration, family disruption, commercial blight, educational failure, and others.

The large-scale unemployment of and lack of socioeconomic mobility by African-Americans during the 1970s and 1980s can also be explained by the ceilings placed by White employers on the mobility of African-American men in male-dominated jobs, and by political disempowerment (Fainstein and Fainstein, 1989). African-American males primarily hold low-wage service jobs, and many hold newly created manufacturing jobs in nonunionized firms, from whom they also receive low wages. Additionally, African-Americans were disproportionately hurt by the policies of the Reagan administration that led to an upward redistribution of power and income within the U.S. class structure. For example, the administration slashed expenditures for moderate-income housing, employment and training, public education, college scholarships, and work-study programs, thereby severing the ladder of opportunity that once extended deep into the minority community.

Due to the pattern of technological change, the future employment prospects for minorities became bleaker. Many minority workers are disproportionately employed in labor-intensive occupations that will continually be the targets of technological change, which causes job displacement and skills disruption. Given that those workers often lack competitive computer and basic technological skills, they are unlikely candidates for job retraining (Wallace, 1989).

Learning occurs within a social context. As individuals grow and mature, they become, in part, a reflection of the sum total of their experiences in society (Jarvis, 1987). The social environments of involuntary minorities are often characterized by unemployment and hyperghettoization in their homes and communities, and by job ceilings and technological displacement in their workplaces. These environments and the learning experiences they foster militate against high rates of participation in adult literacy programs.

Disjunctions Between Primary/Secondary and Nondominant/Dominant Discourses. The culturally informed perspectives of collective minority communities create in involuntary minorities considerable ambivalence toward education. This ambivalence originates in the disjunctive relationship experienced between nondominant and dominant discourses. Gee (1989) explains that discourses are the languages, social roles, attitudes, beliefs, values, and other requirements expected in specific social situations. Through *primary discourses,* which are acquired early in life from the home and peer group, people first make sense of the world and learn how to interact with others. This type of discourse provides a foundation for discourses acquired later in life. For example, the primary discourses of African-Americans are often informed by the concept of "fictive kinship" (Fordham, 1988). Fictive kinship refers to the kinship-like connections among African-Americans not related by blood or marriage, who have maintained essential reciprocal, social, economic, or political relationships.

Secondary discourses are acquired through interactions with various non-home-based institutions located in the public sphere, such as local stores and churches, schools, community groups, and businesses (Gee, 1989). Each social institution commands and demands one or more discourses, and people acquire fluency in the "languages" to the extent that they are given access to these institutions and are allowed apprenticeship within them. Given the social and geographic isolation experienced by involuntary minorities, cultural inversion and fictive kinship systems often serve as secondary discourses.

Gee (1989) also draws an important distinction between *dominant and nondominant discourses.* Dominant discourses are secondary discourses, the mastery of which, at particular places and times, brings the (potential) acquisition of social "goods" (money, prestige, status, and so on). Nondominant discourses, such as fictive kinship ties, are also secondary discourses, the mastery of which often brings solidarity with a particular social network, but not wider status and social goods in the society at large.

Individuals seeking entry into dominant secondary discourses often experience tension and intrapersonal conflict. The tension and conflict are particularly acute when one's primary and secondary nondominant discourses are in opposition to a dominant secondary discourse, for example, the fictive kinship of African-Americans and the dominant secondary discourse of schools. Fordham (1988) argues that this type of conflict is a central impediment to the academic success and socioeconomic mobility of African-Americans. That is, the African-American fictive kinship system is challenged by the individual ethos of the dominant culture when the individuals enter school, and when they experience competition between the two for loyalty.

In response to this tension, one of two strategies is employed. Those African-American students who are sensitive to the marginalized and distorted roles of minorities depicted in American history and literature view the act of attending school as evidence of either a conscious or semiconscious rejection of their primary and secondary nondominant discourses. Therefore, they tend to use Black English vernacular to create an environment that reinforces their fictive kinship identity. Unfortunately, by challenging the dominant discourse in the school setting, they inadvertently ensure their academic failure. Other African-American students seek to minimize their connection to their primary and secondary nondominant discourses and assimilate into the school culture. In order to improve their chances for success in school and in life, these students attempt to develop a "raceless persona" (Fordham, 1988).

Culturally Insensitive Adult Literacy Programs. Adult literacy programs present barriers to minorities when they ignore either the social-structural forces that shape the social context and negative life experiences of many minorities or the disjunctive relationship between the nondominant and dominant secondary discourses often experienced by minorities. They also present serious barriers when they exercise a discourse of "control" that allows teachers to assert their own voices and silence the voices of students (Giroux, 1985). This discourse silences the voices of students by assuming the curriculum is neutral with respect to the depicted images and historical roles of minorities, as evidenced by the uncritical acceptance of published workbooks as the primary curriculum of the program; the failure to gain substantive student input in the determination of the curriculum; and the exclusion of students' personal experiences as components of the curriculum. The discourse of control therefore leads to learning programs that force minority learners to choose between (1) acquiescing to the cultural/literacy demands of mainstream society, thereby losing their cultural heritage and fictive kinship identity and (2) resisting the imposition of the dominant society on their primary and secondary nondominant discourses, thereby losing their access to socioeconomic mobility.

Ideally, adult literacy programs should provide access to socioeconomic mobility without a significant loss of cultural identity. To achieve this goal, practitioners should develop programs that allow teachers to assert their own voices while still encouraging students to affirm, tell, and retell their personal narratives in their own voices (Giroux, 1987). This suggests that teachers should allow students to question the program's most basic assumptions regarding its use of authority. It is through such questioning that students will gain an understanding of how and why such authority is constructed and what purpose it serves.

It appears that some of the school failure experienced by involuntary minorities stems from their uncritical acceptance of cultural inversion as an operative means to combat oppression. It is in response to this perspective that literacy programs should seek to involve involuntary minorities in projects of sociohistorical transformation. Freire and Macedo (1987, p. 65) suggested the feasibility of such projects when they said, "to shape history is to be present in it, not merely represented in it." As conscious beings capable of making and shaping their histories, minorities require dialogical encounters with informative and sensitive teachers and students in an effort to critique the strategy of cultural inversion and identify alternative strategies more conducive to their economic, social and cultural goals.

A Model Adult Literacy Program

My review of the published literature did not yield examples of adult literacy programs that addressed directly the culturally derived barriers cited above. For example, no programs were discovered that were responsive to the cultural inversion perspectives of involuntary minorities. However, one program was identified that proved successful in developing the functional literacy skills of inner-city adults (Bernick, 1986). Although the program, called Tech Prep, reported neither a strong evaluation component (such as the utilization of a control group), an independent evaluator, nor enough details for replication, it does present some positive examples of successful program delivery to culturally unique populations. For example, it responded to the deleterious effects of the low functional skills and the brutal social-structural transformations experienced by inner-city minorities by providing skills training in computer-related technologies.

Tech Prep Course. The Tech Prep course was started in 1983 by the Renaissance job-training and business development corporation, based in San Francisco. In 1982 Renaissance's primary mission was to train unemployed eighteen- to twenty-eight-year-olds in emerging high-technology jobs, such as microcomputer, microwave, and office machine technicians. Renaissance's practitioners found that the majority of the applicants possessed reading and math skills well below the ninth-grade level needed to function in the targeted technical fields. Therefore, the Tech Prep program was initiated to raise the skills of applicants who were at the sixth- and seventh-grade levels to the eighth- and ninth-grade levels required by the technical jobs they aspired to fill. The three-month program included both high school noncompleters and graduates and led participants into technician training, into other advanced vocational training, or directly into jobs.

Participants were recruited through flyers, radio advertisements, and word of mouth. Although the applicants were not provided stipends, they were promised that if they took the course seriously, either they would be admitted into the Renaissance technician-training program or else jobs would be found for them. Applicants were asked to sign contracts in which they agreed to attend every class, to be on time, to work to the best of their abilities, and to keep a positive attitude.

Each session of the course consisted of two hours of reading and writing and one hour of math. The sessions took place five days a week. The traditional classroom instruction was supplemented by the use of microcomputers and a variety of software educational programs to practice reading comprehension and basic math. The class also included discussions of the environment in the workplace and of such job-search skills as resume writing, job searching, and interviewing.

Of seventeen students, thirteen completed the course. Of the seven high school noncompleters, six obtained their diplomas by passing the GED test. The three months of coursework were not sufficient to bring the students' functional skills up to the level required to conduct most business correspondence or written transactions. However, on Tests of Adult Basic Education, they showed gains in both vocabulary and comprehension ranging from one to three years. Seven of the students entered advanced vocational training, three took entry-level jobs, one entered college, and one entered an engineering training program.

Program Components Linked to Success. Several structural components and classroom environment characteristics of the program appeared to facilitate its success with this population:

1. *Diagnostic assessment.* Given that no culturally unbiased tests are currently on the market, testing served the two purposes of determining the nature of the students' academic difficulties and measuring progress. Students were tested when they entered the program and subsequently.

2. *Focus on basic skills and problem solving.* The instruction focused on the development of functional skills in reading, writing, math, and problem solving. It was characterized by an intense focus on the subject matter, with no electives or distractions, and drew heavily on the students' own experiences. For example, if the students read an essay on the differences between common sense and college education, it was followed by a group discussion of different types of education. The teacher listed ideas on the chalkboard and asked the students to write one-page essays. These types of exercises provided the students with opportunities for analyzing subjects, developing new ideas, and expressing them in writing.

3. *Classroom atmosphere.* Each instructor was assigned only one class; therefore, she or he fostered strong interpersonal relationships with students and among students.

4. *Computer-assisted instruction.* Computers were used to complement

the traditional instruction, help students to develop their computer literacy skills, and allow them to proceed at their own pace.

5. *Connection to the work environment.* Because the program held the promise of either technical training or a job, students could see the proverbial light at the end of the tunnel.

Like many such programs in the inner city, the Tech Prep program experienced major funding problems. It has survived by means of several foundation and government-training grants but has received no public education funds.

Conclusion

Relentless negative social-structural forces and the deep disjunction between the secondary (nondominate) discourses of nonvoluntary minorities and the secondary (dominate) discourses of the dominate culture create for involuntary minorities both external and internal barriers to their efforts to fulfill the promise of our constitutional democracy, that is, to "earn a living" and to "live well." Although these are two of the basic freedoms granted in the U.S. Constitution, their attainment is denied to a disproportionate number of minorities who must confront the effects of hyperghettoization in their neighborhoods and home environments, racism and job ceilings in the workplace, and their own uncritical acceptance of "cultural inversion" as an operative means to combat an oppressive society. Although the Tech Prep course provides an effective model to address some of the "instrumental" learning needs of specific segments of inner-city minority communities, too many other literacy programs fail to specifically address the literacy needs of involuntary minorities. These minorities require culturally sensitive learning environments that present opportunities to critically reflect on and to transform both the social-structural forces that affect their lives and their own personal histories and perspectives that could lead to an uncritical acceptance of cultural inversion. Not until adult literacy programs empower learners to become critically reflective citizens of our democracy will they fulfill their promise to both society and their students of providing a last chance to acquire the values, attitudes, skills, knowledge, and perspectives needed to both "earn a living" and to "live well."

References

Bernick, M. "Illiteracy and Inner-City Unemployment." *Phi Delta Kappan,* 1986, *67* (5), 364–367.

Fainstein, S., and Fainstein, N. I. "The Racial Dimensions in Urban Political Economy." *Urban Affairs Quarterly,* 1989, *25* (2), 187–199.

Fordham, S. "Racelessness as a Factor in Black Students' School Success: Pragmatic Strategy or Pyrrhic Victory?" *Harvard Educational Review,* 1988, *58* (1), 54–84.

Freire, P., and Macedo, D. (eds.). *Literacy: Reading the Word and the World.* South Hadley, Mass.: Bergin and Garvey, 1987.

Gee, P. J. "Literacy, Discourse, and Linguistics: Introduction." *Journal of Education,* 1989, *171* (1), 5-17.

Giroux, H. "Critical Pedagogy, Cultural Politics, and the Discourse of Experience." *Journal of Education,* 1985, *167* (2), 22-41.

Giroux, H. "Introduction: Literacy and the Pedagogy of Political Empowerment." In P. Freire and D. Macedo (eds.), *Literacy: Reading the Word and the World.* South Hadley, Mass.: Bergin and Garvey, 1987.

Hayes, E. R., and Darkenwald, G. "Participation in Basic Education: Deterrents for Low-Literate Adults." *Studies in the Education of Adults,* 1988, *20* (1), 16-28.

Jarvis, P. *Adult Learning in the Social Context.* New York: Croom Helm, 1987.

Kirsch, I., and Jungeblut, A. *Literacy: Profiles of America's Young Adults.* Final report no. 16-PL-01. Princeton, N.J.: National Assessment of Educational Progress, 1986.

Malizio, A. G., and Whitney, D. R. *Who Takes the GED Tests? A National Survey of Spring 1980 Examinees.* Washington, D.C.: American Council on Education, 1981.

National Center for Education Statistics. *Digest of Education Statistics.* Office of Educational Research and Improvement and the National Center for Education Statistics. Washington, D.C.: Government Printing Office, 1988.

Ogbu, J. "Minority Status and Literacy in Comparative Perspective." *Daedalus,* 1990, *119* (2), 141-168.

Pugsley, R. *National Data Update—Annual Conference: State Directors of Adult Education.* Division of Adult Education, U.S. Department of Education. Washington, D.C.: Government Printing Office, 1987.

Wacquant, L. D., and Wilson, W. J. "The Cost of Racial and Class Exclusion in the Inner City." *Annals of the American Academy of Political and Social Science* (special issue, *The Ghetto Underclass: Social Science Perspectives*), 1989, *501*, 8-25.

Wallace, M. "Brave New Workplace: Technology and Work in the New Economy." *Work and Occupations,* 1989, *16* (4), 363-392.

Larry G. Martin is associate professor of adult and continuing education at the University of Wisconsin, Milwaukee. He has published extensively on issues concerning the empowerment of educationally disenfranchised groups through adult literacy education.

At the end of the twentieth century, American society and higher education face demographic and cultural problems similar to those experienced at the end of the nineteenth century.

Education, Democracy, and Cultural Pluralism: Continuing Higher Education in an Age of Diversity

John F. Moe

The connections between education and democracy have long been at the heart of the founding precepts of American society. Indeed, the success of the American experiment is often measured by the extent to which our society's citizens are included in its educational institutions (Bok, 1982; Cremin, 1977, 1980). The fabric of U.S. history is interlaced with chronicles of newly arrived immigrants who struggled and sacrificed to attend and complete school. During the nineteenth and twentieth centuries, these new populations in American higher education included the new European immigrants, first men and then women, and, finally, minorities. To a great degree, the historical literature of each population group focused on the importance of education for economic success and social acceptance into the mainstream of American society. Now, at the conclusion of the twentieth century, the evolving definitions of democracy and education assume critical proportions as American society embarks on a new stage of cultural pluralism.

This chapter calls attention to some of the issues facing educators who work in institutions that are being challenged to embrace an increasingly diverse American population. Embedded in the argument presented here is the idea that the tripartite arrangement of education, democracy,

The author thanks Paula C. Baker and Jovita M. Ross-Gordon for their assistance in the preparation of this chapter.

and cultural pluralism is critical to understanding both the past and the present of the educational system in America and that this tripartite arrangement will determine the future success of American higher education. The chapter begins by examining some of the historical and demographic trends that affect our understanding of cultural pluralism in American society and continues by describing programmatic solutions posed by selected educational institutions in the United States. Finally, the chapter attempts to pose some questions and answers to the continuing dilemmas, challenges, and opportunities that are inherent to cultural pluralism and change in our society.

The American Melting Pot, Citizenry, and Education

Fundamental to an understanding of American social development is the process of immigration described throughout the late nineteenth and early twentieth centuries as the American "Melting Pot." Education was viewed by both immigrants and the proponents of immigration as the primary means for immigrant groups to enter the democratic process and claim their places in American society. At the end of the nineteenth century, women, African-Americans, and European immigrants sought to acquire education, and its attendant skills and tools, that would equip them in their efforts to assume their rightful places within society. As each successive wave of immigrants entered the United States, inclusion in the education system became a paramount concern for the new population. At the turn of the century, the last vestiges of the "old immigration" and the large numbers of the "new immigration" flooded onto the American scene, forever changing its landscape and social institutions (Jones, 1960, pp. 177-206).

The relative success of creating a new, culturally pluralistic society that included the early European immigrants was clear and demonstrable. At the end of the nineteenth century, the country was infused with groups that would complement, and antagonize, the "host" immigrants who had arrived earlier. The new immigrants, including large numbers of Italians and Eastern Europeans, joined the old immigrant groups of English, German, Irish, Scandinavian, and other Western Europeans to form, if not a "Melting Pot," a culturally pluralistic society. Jacob Riis, a Danish immigrant to New York City, recognized this aspect of the American landscape in his book *How the Other Half Lives: Studies Among the Tenements of New York.* "A map of the city," wrote Riis in 1890, "coloured to designate nationality, would show more stripes than on the skin of a zebra, and more colours than any rainbow" (Riis, 1957, p. 18). Aside from his criticism of the class-ridden society, Riis's assessment of a culturally pluralistic nation certainly resembles the United States of 1990.

The traditional view of each of the European immigrant groups espoused the notion that education was essential for immigrant success in the new democracy. The historical literature of the various immigrant groups tended, in the older school of immigration history, to emphasize each group's contribution to American democracy. These histories chronicled the travails and family sacrifices of the new immigrants and focused on education as a means of insuring success in the United States.

Oscar Handlin, perhaps the best-known American immigration historian, drew a solid connection between the concepts of democracy, education, and cultural pluralism in his important immigration history of the United States, *The Uprooted*. In his chapter "Democracy and Power," Handlin points to the demands of citizenry as a force in the immigrant's acquisition of power. "Having settled and survived the five years, the newcomer was expected to become a citizen" (Handlin, 1951, p. 205). Handlin notes, however, that formal education for many immigrants was counterproductive. American school readers of the late nineteenth century focused on the image of the old immigrants, that is, the Western Europeans, thus denying the new immigrants their own cultural legacies. "That was an additional reason why the immigrants labored to create educational institutions of their own; they hoped thereby to minimize the contest" (1951, p. 244).

Two developments occurred during the last decade of the nineteenth century and the first decade of the twentieth that enabled recent immigrants, including African-Americans, to create educational institutions of their own, thereby posing a solution to the difficulties raised by the domination of the culture by the old immigrants. The first was the growth of ethnic newspapers, and the second was the development of schools specifically designated for particular cultural groups. These two institutions helped preserve the cultural and ethnic identities of "new" immigrants and, at the same time, contributed to relatively safe and comfortable transitions from their former lives.

Probably the most pervasive adult education tool during the period from 1880 to 1910 was the newspaper. Nearly every immigrant group from Europe had a newspaper, which, in Handlin's terms, minimized the contest with the host culture and served as a safe haven for the immigrant readers. Newly formed African-American communities in the North during the 1890s and after maintained a similarly viable and active press. The ethnic press allowed its readers to enhance their potential for citizenry and provided to them a positive sense of their own cultural legacies (Handlin, 1951; Thornbrough, 1972).

This same time period also witnessed the growth of a traditional European folk school movement in the United States (Moe, 1984, p. 125). The idea of residential adult education, particularly successful in Scandinavia and England, was brought to the United States during the early years of the twentieth century. The ethnic folk school served as a means of enhancing an ethnic group's cultural distinctiveness and legacy through a familiar means of adult education. For example, in September 1903, the Finnish

Evangelical Lutheran National Church sponsored the founding of a folk high school in Minneapolis, Minnesota. Later moved to Duluth, the school offered Finnish immigrants instruction in religion and in Finnish culture and nationalism.

Ethnic newspapers and ethnic schools forestalled the societal tensions of the mid-twentieth century by taking immigrant populations out of the mainstream. As long as each group's ethnic and cultural legacy was preserved, the battle for survival was minimally successful. The consequences of this tension are still being resolved at the end of the twentieth century. Since the 1960s, the institutions that provided immigrants with safe havens from the rest of society (for example, Black Masons or the Danish Hall) have begun to disappear or have disappeared altogether.

Demographics of a Culturally Diverse Adult Population

Implicit in an understanding of the impact of the American educational system is the question of access to educational institutions. Kramer (1989) provides an informative analysis of this question in his article on education in a multicultural society. Throughout the nineteenth and twentieth centuries, each immigrant group recognized the importance of education, in general, and adult education, in particular. Efforts by immigrants to achieve full citizenship, the development of ethnic newspapers and folk schools, and sacrifices by individual families all pointed to the deep need in our democratic society for educational attainment. The lessons learned by previous immigrant groups have not been lost on contemporary immigrants, including new arrivals from Asia and the Caribbean and recent Jewish emigrés from the Soviet Union.

These efforts within ethnic communities to acquire and share knowledge and skills notwithstanding, the minority adult population in the United States today has not acquired equal access to higher education and has not been sufficiently included in the design of adult education programs made available through institutions of higher education (Arbeiter, 1987; Atwell, 1988; Briscoe and Ross, 1989; College Entrance Examination Board, 1985; Loo and Rolison, 1986; Moe, 1989; Nettles, Thoeny, and Gosman, 1986; Richardson, 1989; Ross, 1988; Santos and Richardson, 1988). In order to fulfill the promise of education in a democratic society based on cultural pluralism, it is important that all citizens be served by society's institutions of higher education. Educational service in a multicultural, democratic society implies equal opportunity and respect for the diverse cultural heritages of individuals and communities.

The Second World War marked a new period of influx of adult students into higher education. The end of the war brought a new clientele into the student ranks of U.S. colleges and universities, significantly altering the mission and climate of higher education (Moe, 1989, p. 35). Institutions of higher learning have, to a great extent, overcome the exclusion of women and ethnic Europeans, including the Jewish populations, from the student pool. Participation by the traditional-aged and adult minority student populations, however, lags far behind. An overview of the demographic issues related to minority adult participation in higher education may help clarify some of the questions related to how educational programs can serve an increasingly culturally diverse adult population.

Most publicity and policy research on educational attainment have largely ignored adult students. Perhaps the pattern of attainment by traditional-aged students is more readily understood by the public, and the statistics related to their progress may seem more vital to the health of the nation. While reliable national data on educational attainment by minority students (particularly American Indians, Asians, African-Americans, and Hispanics) are relatively scarce, some published information is available.

A brief look at school completion rates by race at the secondary level helps explain patterns of attainment by adults in institutions of higher education. The Office of Educational Research Improvement of the U.S. Department of Education reports that, during the past ten years, the dropout rates for Whites and Blacks declined, with the dropout rate for Blacks in 1988 declining to a level only slightly higher than that of Whites. The dropout rate for Hispanics, however, remains high and has not changed significantly for fifteen years. In 1988, almost one-third of Hispanics aged sixteen to twenty-four were neither enrollees in school nor high school graduates. Hispanics were six times more likely than Whites and Blacks to have no more than an elementary education (U.S. Department of Education, 1989).

Recent national data indicate that marked disparities between White and minority adults still persist in attainment in higher education. The U.S. Bureau of the Census (1988) Current Population Survey examined the years of college completed by adults twenty-five years of age and older, compiling percentages distributed by sex and by race and ethnicity for 1987. While 11.5 percent of these adults reported completion of four years of college, there were clear race differences in educational attainment. Nearly 12 percent of Whites finished college, while less than 7 percent of Black adults in this age group completed four years of college. The discrepancy between college completion by Whites and by Hispanics was even greater, with only about 5 percent of adults of Hispanic origin reporting completion of four years of college. Despite the U.S. Department of Education report that 1988 enrollments for all minorities showed significant increases from 1986 levels, the absolute levels of attainment by Hispanic adults remain low (Evangelauf, 1990). The U.S. Bureau of the Census (1988) report also indicates that percentages for American Indians were negligible to the point of unreliability. A more recent report, describing demographic and economic characteristics of American Indian tribes as of 1980, indicates that 7.7 percent of

Indians completed four or more years of college. This report was based on sample estimates (U.S. Bureau of the Census, 1990).

While these census data are important for assessing higher education attainment in the overall adult population, additional insights emerge from examination of finer age categorization of the data. For example, differences in college completion by race appear to diminish at younger adult age levels. Among Blacks, the percentage of men completing the fourth year of college drops from just over 9 percent in the age category of twenty-five- to twenty-nine-year-olds, to under 4 percent in the age category of fifty- to fifty-five-year-olds. Similarly, college completion rates for Black women drop from 9 percent to about 6 percent between the same two age categories. The magnitude of this difference is moderated by the fact that among whites and Hispanics, there are comparable drops in percentages.

Some of these differences in educational attainment may be artifacts of the self-report technique used for data collection among older adult respondents. For example, whether through faulty recall or perceived social desirability, older adults may significantly exaggerate their respective levels of educational attainment, compared to what younger adults report. (Future research is planned that compares differences in educational attainment by sex and by race and ethnicity utilizing the five-year-interval categories of the U.S. Census Bureau. For the ages between twenty-five years and seventy-five years, an investigation of five-year intervals should yield more specific profiles of the population's educational attainment.) Nonetheless, real and significant disparities exist in the overall U.S. educational profile when comparing college completion rates by sex and by race and ethnicity. These data are important since they represent the composite adult population from which universities and colleges are attempting to recruit and retain minority adult students (Ross, 1988, 1989).

The U.S. Bureau of the Census (1988) also presents data on completion rates for the fourth year of college by adults twenty-five years of age and older, by sex and by race and ethnicity, for the years 1986 and 1987. Completion rates of the fourth year of college by Whites remained approximately the same over the two-year span. The overall completion rate for Hispanics increased slightly by .2 percent. In comparison, the percentage for Black adults declined by .4 percent. This drop may be accounted for by the fact that while attendance rates remained relatively steady over the two years, there was a decline in the proportion graduating. Traditionally, elitist admissions standards have helped ensure a relatively high graduation rate. As more students with varying degrees of readiness and preparation attend college, one would expect to see some decline in graduation rates.

Racial differences in median school years completed were also evidenced, with 12.7 median years completed for Whites, 12.4 for Blacks, and 12 for Hispanics. It is interesting that Blacks of both sexes showed comparable levels of median years of school completion (12.4) and participation in college until the junior and senior years, when female enrollment appears to drop. Men in all racial groups reported higher levels of college completion, and indeed retention prior to graduation. The patterns of college completion and median school years completed by Hispanics are particularly troublesome. Female Hispanics were particularly underrepresented as college graduates, with slightly more than 4 percent reporting college completion in 1986, and well under 5 percent indicating they completed college in 1987.

Comparing completion rates of four years of college or more by racial and ethnic groups for 1980 and 1987, the U.S. Bureau of the Census (1988) figures for Whites and Blacks echo trends discussed earlier. Increases for these two groups proceeded at approximately the same rate, while the figures for the Hispanic population indicate that this group lagged behind in all categories of educational attainment. Whereas educational attainment for Whites and Blacks increased by about 3 percent between 1980 and 1987, attainment for Hispanics over the same period increased only .7 percent. The importance of these data are that they span nearly a decade of concentration on the problems of minority educational attainment. Thus, while the trends for both White and Black adults are somewhat encouraging, the educational attainment data for Hispanics during this same time period are clearly discouraging.

Some Programmatic Conclusions: American Education in an Age of New Diversity

A key issue in American public education today is the design and implementation of educational programs that both equip students with knowledge and skills and maintain respect for the cultural legacies and histories of individuals and groups. What European immigrant groups sought to perpetuate in the nineteenth and early twentieth centuries with ethnic newspapers and ethnic folk schools remains a viable objective today. Among minority groups, as well as women, educational participation and attainment are critical for survival in the larger society, but only within a framework that acknowledges the value of individual and cultural identity.

While the college enrollment and completion rates of minority adults persist at levels below those of the general population, certain social and economic forces may lead to increased minority and female adult participation in higher education. Job performance, technological change in the workplace, life transitions, part-time graduate study, expanded free time, and a lessening of the negative image associated with attending college in adulthood are factors that appear to contribute to increased adult participation in higher education (Apps, 1988; Brookfield, 1985; Darkenwald and Merriam, 1982; Lynton and Elman, 1987; Ross, 1989; Soedjatmoko, 1989).

Nonetheless, it is clear that minority participation in higher education and in education in general has not achieved the success heralded by an aggressively multicultural society (Warren, 1990). DePalma (1990) notes that Blacks, Hispanics, and Asians will comprise a third of the nation's public school students by the year 2000: "Their numbers will present challenges unlike anything most states have seen since the great migrations of the turn of the [last] century." Indeed, the challenges of nineteenth-century migration and the responses of immigrants to relocation offer hints to adult and continuing educators about what needs should be addressed in new programs designed to assist and educate American minority students.

Serving a Culturally Diverse Adult Population in Higher Education

Clearly, most observers of adult and higher education have noted the increased pressure from both inside and outside minority communities to widen the scope of the adult student pool. Warren (1990) notes that minorities are projected to comprise over 50 percent of the total U.S. population by the year 2050. Minorities will inherit the reins of power in much the same way that earlier immigrant populations assumed them in the twentieth century. He notes that unless educational opportunities are created for contemporary minorities, they will enter the twenty-first century unprepared for leadership. The repercussions of such neglect can already be seen in the growing size and problems of the U.S. underclass. Warren contends that what is at stake is the very future of the United States. He speaks specifically to the needs of American Indians when he proposes that programs be built around their cultural legacy and history in ways that echo the establishment of immigrant institutions in the late nineteenth century (Warren, personal communication, 1988–1990).

Several colleges and universities are responding to the pressures for increased minority enrollment by structuring programs aimed at elementary and secondary school students. Such efforts, however, have not been joined with complementary efforts to bring minority adults to the college and university campuses. Recruitment and retention of both young and adult minorities remain persistent problems within institutions of higher learning. Indeed, as Kramer (1989, p. 2) suggests, "more is known about those dimensions of institutional environment which discourage minority participation than we know about those which engender it."

In response to the growing need for minority adult participation in higher education, the Office of Continuing Education at Ohio State University developed the innovative Minority Continuing Education Opportunity Program (MCEOP) as part of its commitment to minority adult continuing education. MCEOP, which is specifically intended to attract minority adults to the undergraduate and graduate programs of the university, involves an alliance among the university, local corporations and businesses, and the students to guarantee the highest possible chance for student success.

Fully operational since 1986, MCEOP has successfully confronted the range of adult student needs: accurate academic assessment, effective tutorial assistance, adequate financial assistance, personalized admission procedures, and an environment that offers social and academic support. Admission into the program involves a unique interplay between the university and places of student employment. "Corporate recommendations rather than test scores or prior education records are employed to identify prospective students. The program admits students whose potential for and interest in learning has been documented in the workplace and whose career circumstances may be enhanced as a consequence of university enrollment" (Kramer, 1989, p. 4).

The program is designed to provide academic, financial, and social assistance tailored to the minority clientele that it serves. Academic tutoring and support, provided in individual settings, is designed to address issues and situations of university life in general and those unique to minorities in particular. A critical feature of MCEOP is the "recyclable tuition program," in which the university pays a student's fees in advance of course completion and is then reimbursed by the corporation employing the student. The recyclable tuition monies enable students to begin course work without the burden of significant financial investment. Corporate reimbursement to the program is completed when the student completes the courses. The program has proved quite effective in providing minority adult students with a sound infrastructure that supports them academically, socially, and financially. To date the program has experienced virtually a 100 percent success rate in student retention.

Recognizing Diversity in a Democracy

The commonality that appears to exist between the multicultural society of the late nineteenth century and the multicultural society of the late twentieth century can be summarized by the idea of diversity as the central basis of unity. Indeed, within the vast range of our multicultural society, individuals are seen as exhibiting unique qualities while at the same time reflecting the larger society, the diversity of their surroundings. One measure of societal success during this new stage of cultural pluralism will be the degree to which U.S. social policies address the serious problems of illiteracy, unemployment, homelessness, poverty, and group disenfranchisement while maintaining respect for individual and group cultural identity.

The question of minority adult participation in education plays a pivotal role in addressing and solving these social problems. Studies reported in *Black Issues in Higher Education* indicate that adult and continuing education programs are not reaching minority populations, a contention supported by statistics from the U.S. Department of Education. While the minority perception of predominantly White campuses as alien environments remains an important impediment to minority enrollment, financial aid is seen as the biggest obstacle to continuing education's minority recruitment (O'Brien, 1990, pp. 6-7).

Just as folk schools created a learning and social environment for Scandinavian immigrant education in the United States at the end of the last century, so too must contemporary educational institutions create a new learning and social setting if they are to attract adult minority students. As the folk schools of nearly a century ago were largely successful in addressing many of their contemporary social problems, colleges and universities will have to formulate new ways of reducing institutional barriers to student diversity and minority retention in order to alleviate twentieth-century social problems.

Design of the Navajo Community College. The design of the Navajo Community College in Chinle, Arizona, illustrates an effort to make education relevant to minority student needs. When the decision was made to create the college, planners, including both professionals and American Indians from the community, asked a fundamental question: "What is Navajo education?" They turned to Navajo culture, folklore, and history for the answers. The resultant educational setting, including both the curriculum and the architecture of the school, reflects Navajo values and history. An effort was made to provide a comfortable place in which to study, regardless of whether the individual Navajo student chose to live inside or outside the reservation (Dean Jackson, personal communication, 1988–1989). Today, the administration building, the classroom buildings and dormitories, and the religious building resemble the architecture of the traditional Navajo hogan. Clearly, the physical environment of the community college has been designed to reaffirm the cultural legacy of its students.

Analogous to the builders of the Finnish folk schools in Minnesota, the designers of the Navajo Community College and its curriculum recognized the importance of providing an education responsive to the interconnections of individual and community in Navajo culture. Educational administrators and planners who work with American Indian students emphasize the importance of cultural diversity in developing programs that respond to Indian needs and that encourage the participation of Indians in higher education (Warren, 1990).

Smithsonian Museum of the American Indian. For the new Smithsonian Museum of the American Indian, efforts are being made to create educational programs that are both culturally relevant and accessible to all citizens of the American Indian community, particularly the often-excluded adult population (Warren, 1990). Warren has proposed that in order to accomplish the museum's objectives, the programs must exploit contemporary technologies to deliver educational services to the remote geographical locations in which many American Indians live. Warren raises issues that educators in general have stressed in dealing with the problems inherent to providing education to adult minority students. Institutions of higher learning can alter their patterns of educational delivery in order to reach segments of the population not adequately served.

Conclusions: Education and the American Melting Pot

Contemporary immigrant literature is replete with narratives that emphasize the importance of education in achieving success in the United States. It must be remembered that of the many groups who immigrated to the United States, some came more willingly than others. Nonetheless, the immigrant literature of the nineteenth and twentieth centuries is a catalogue of immigrant responses to the avenues of understanding and acceptance in American society. In a chronicle of his family's immigration from Puerto Rico to New York, Edward Rivera recounts his family's insistence that he attend school, learn English, and do well in his studies in order to succeed in their new country. His brother tells him, "Listen Santos, don't do like me, man. I made a big mistake not working harder when I was in Santa Misweria's [the Catholic school]. I wouldn't be in the dump I'm in now [if I had done well in school]" (Rivera, 1982, p. 133).

Literature from other immigrant groups can be cited that describes the link between educational achievement and success in American society, for example, Rølvaag's (1987) chronicle of Norwegian immigration. Whatever the details of each case-in-point, this idea of education in a democracy is the thread that unites the various elements of a culturally pluralistic society into what has been termed the Melting Pot. The mythology of the Melting Pot has led to frustrations among immigrant groups who assumed that education would enable them to succeed in society.

The idea of the Melting Pot has been attacked in the historical literature. For example, Carl Degler (1959, p. 295) has noted that in 1908, at the height of the last great surge of immigration, "a naive and sentimental play about American immigrants, written by an English Jew, captured the imaginations of American theatergoers." *The Melting Pot*, by Israel Zangwill, has become immortalized in the minds of students of American thought and history as a symbol of the social aspect of the American Dream. "There she lies, the great Melting Pot," exclaimed the hero of the play, "East and West, and North and South, the palm and the pine, the pole and the equator, the crescent and the cross—how the great Alchemist melts and fuses them with his purging flames" (Degler, 1959, pp. 295-296). Degler (1959, p. 296), citing the panorama of languages and styles of the immigrants, contended that the "metaphor of the melting pot is unfortunate and misleading. A more accurate analogy would be a salad bowl, for, though the salad is an entity, the lettuce can still be distinguished from the chicory, the tomatoes from the cabbage."

Current observers echo Degler's image of an entity with distinct elements. Ravitch (1990, p. 18) notes that "we are a multicultural people, but also a single nation knitted together by a common set of political and moral values." She poses a question salient to contemporary minority adult higher education: How do we ensure that education promotes pluralism? If one of the key issues in American higher education is the development of programs that maintain respect for the diverse cultures of individuals and communities, then the issues attendant to the tripartite connection between education, democracy, and cultural pluralism will have to be identified by educators who prepare programs for adult and continuing education. These programs, like the historical models and current programs discussed here, must recognize diversity as a basis for unity in an age of democracy. Moreover, educational programs designed to enhance cultural diversity will serve minority populations in reclaiming as well as maintaining cultural legacies. Lost and forgotten parts of the cultures of African-Americans, Hispanic Americans, Asian-Americans, American Indians, and other minority groups should be included in new educational plans as a means of contributing to the cultural diversity of the United States.

References

Apps, J. W. *Higher Education in a Learning Society: Meeting New Demands for Education and Training.* San Francisco: Jossey-Bass, 1988.
Arbeiter, S. "Black Enrollments: The Case of the Missing Students." *Change,* 1987, *19* (3), 14-19.
Atwell, R. H. *Minority Participation in Higher Education: We Need a New Momentum.* Washington, D.C.: American Council on Education, 1988.
Bok, D. *Beyond the Ivory Tower: Social Responsibilities of the Modern University.* Cambridge, Mass.: Harvard University Press, 1982.
Briscoe, D. B., and Ross, J. M. "Racial and Ethnic Minorities and Adult Education." In S. B. Merriam and P. M. Cunningham (eds.), *Handbook of Adult and Continuing Education.* San Francisco: Jossey-Bass, 1989.
Brookfield, S. D. "A Critical Definition of Adult Education." *Adult Education Quarterly,* 1985, *36* (1), 44-49.
College Entrance Examination Board. *Equality and Excellence: The Educational Status of Black Americans.* New York: College Entrance Examination Board, 1985.
Cremin, L. A. *Traditions of American Education.* New York: Basic Books, 1977.
Cremin, L. A. *American Education: The National Experience, 1783-1876.* New York: Harper & Row, 1980.
Darkenwald, G. G., and Merriam, S. B. *Adult Education: Foundations of Practice.* New York: Harper & Row, 1982.
Degler, C. N. *Out of Our Past. The Forces That Shaped Modern America.* New York: Harper & Row, 1959.
DePalma, A. "A House Divided." *New York Times,* Apr. 8, 1990, section 4A, p. 31.
Evangelauf, J. "1988 Enrollments of All Racial Groups Hit Record Levels." *Chronicle of Higher Education,* Apr. 11, 1990, pp. A1, A37.

Handlin, O. *The Uprooted.* Boston: Houghton Mifflin, 1951.

Jones, M. A. *American Immigration.* Chicago: University of Chicago Press, 1960.

Kramer, J. L. "Continuing Education in a Multicultural Society: Challenges of Access and Environment." *Journal of Continuing Higher Education,* 1989, *37* (1), 2–4.

Loo, C. M., and Rolison, G. "Alienation of Ethnic Minority Students at a Predominantly White University." *Journal of Higher Education,* 1986, *57* (1), 58–77.

Lynton, E. A., and Elman, S. E. *New Priorities for the University: Meeting Society's Needs for Applied Knowledge and Competent Individuals.* San Francisco: Jossey-Bass, 1987.

Moe, J. F. "Overview: Dimensions of Residential Adult Education from Folk Schools to University Conference Centers." *Continuum,* 1984, *48* (2), 123–129.

Moe, J. F. "The Dream Deferred: Minority Adult Participation in Higher Education in the United States." *Continuing Higher Education Review,* 1989, *52* (1), 35–49.

Nettles, M. T., Thoeny, A. R., and Gosman, E. J. "Comparative and Predictive Analyses of Black and White Students' College Achievement and Experiences." *Journal of Higher Education,* 1986, *57* (3), 289–318.

O'Brien, E. M. "Continuing Ed Programs Not Reaching Minority Populations, Officials Admit." *Black Issues in Higher Education,* Mar. 1, 1990, pp. 6–8.

Ravitch, D. "Diversity and Democracy: Multicultural Education in America." *American Educator,* 1990, *14* (1), 16–20, 46–48.

Richardson, R. C., Jr. "If Minority Students Are to Succeed in Higher Education, Every Rung of the Educational Ladder Must Be in Place." *Chronicle of Higher Education,* Jan. 11, 1989, p. A48.

Riis, J. *How the Other Half Lives: Studies Among the Tenements of New York.* New York: Hill and Wang, 1957. (Originally published 1890.)

Rivera, E. *Family Installments: Memories of Growing Up Hispanic.* New York: William Morrow, 1982.

Rølvaag, O. *The Third Life of Per Smevik.* New York: Harper & Row, 1987. (Originally published 1912.)

Ross, J. M. "Needed Research in Adult Education: A Multicultural Perspective." Paper presented at the annual meeting of the Commission of Professors of Adult Education, Tulsa, Oklahoma, November 1, 1988.

Ross, J. M. "Recruiting and Retaining Adult Students in Higher Education." In P. S. Cookson (ed.), *Recruiting and Retaining Adult Students.* New Directions for Continuing Education, no. 41. San Francisco: Jossey-Bass, 1989.

Santos, A., Jr., and Richardson, R. C., Jr. "Ten Principles for Good Institutional Practice in Removing Race/Ethnicity as a Factor in College Completion." *Educational Record,* 1988, *69* (3/4), 43–47.

Soedjatmoko. "Education Relevant to People's Needs." *Daedalus,* 1989, *118* (1), 211–218.

Thornbrough, E. L. T. *Thomas Fortune: Militant Journalist.* Chicago: University of Chicago Press, 1972.

U.S. Bureau of the Census. *Educational Attainment in the United States: March 1986 and 1987.* Current Population Report, Series P-20, no. 428. Washington, D.C.: Government Printing Office, 1988.

U.S. Bureau of the Census. *Characteristics of American Indians by Tribes and Selected Areas: 1980.* PC80-2-1C. Washington, D.C.: Government Printing Office, 1990.

U.S. Department of Education. *Minority Student Issues: Racial/Ethnic Data Collected by the National Center for Education Statistics Since 1969.* Office of Educational Research and Improvement, CS 89-267. Washington, D.C.: Government Printing Office, 1989.

Warren, D. "Continuity of Heritage and the Creation of Vision: Dimensions of a Multicultural Life." Paper presented at the National University Continuing Education Association Conference, New Orleans, May 1, 1990.

John F. Moe is currently Fulbright professor of American Studies at the University of Bergen in Bergen, Norway (1990–1991). He is associate director of continuing education and adjunct associate professor of art education and museum studies in the College of Art at Ohio State University, Columbus, and serves on the board of directors of the National University Continuing Education Association (1989–1991).

New demographic realities and other significant workplace trends increasingly will require human resource professionals to address problems and issues that relate to diversity.

Cultural Diversity in the Workplace: Managing a Multicultural Work Force

Larry G. Martin, Jovita M. Ross-Gordon

Both the U.S. population and its work force are growing more slowly than at any time since the 1930s (Goddard, 1989). The average age of the pool of young workers entering the labor market is shrinking, and minorities are representing a larger share of new labor market participants. For the first time in U.S. history, demographic profiles of the work force indicate that White males are the minority—only 46 percent (Copeland, 1988). However, racial and ethnic minorities are projected to constitute 29 percent of labor force entrants between now and the year 2000, twice the current percentage. Also, an additional 400,000 legal and illegal immigrants are projected to enter the U.S. work force annually through the balance of the century, and they will compose the largest share of immigrants in the work force since World War I (Goddard, 1989).

The workers projected to enter the work force will be vastly different from the highly educated and acculturated White male workers who have dominated the work force in the past. Employers must adjust not only to new demographic realities but to other significant trends as well, such as technological innovations and increased global competition. These trends encourage employers to increasingly depend on the skills of all their employees for improvements in efficiency, quality, and customer service, and for development of new applications for existing products and services. This increasing reliance on human capital in the workplace is on a collision course with the emerging demographic reality in the United States; that is, future workers will be drawn from populations traditionally unprepared for work, possibly resulting in a decline in both the quantity and quality of human resources available for entry-level jobs.

Human resource professionals will likely be challenged by managers to provide innovative approaches to both solving culturally induced organizational problems and meeting the workplace learning needs of minority individuals and groups in order to keep the organizations competitive in a turbulent and highly competitive global marketplace. This task is made more difficult because the types of jobs created by the economy will demand much higher levels of skill than jobs existing today. Minority workers not only are less likely to have had adequate pre-employment education and on-the-job training, but they also may have language patterns, attitudes, and cultural perspectives that differ significantly from those of existing employees. These differences could arouse in existing employees counterproductive attitudes and behaviors that inhibit the development of a productive work force. Employers should begin investing now in education, training, and other efforts to manage diversity in order to secure a productive and competitive work force in the future. This chapter provides the human resource professional with an overview of the potential problems and opportunities that are likely to accompany a more culturally diverse workplace.

Minority Participation in the Work Force

Since this country's inception, minorities have made significant contributions to its work force. However, the proportion of minorities participating in the work force has varied considerably over time. According to the Bureau of the Census, the U.S. labor force increased significantly from nearly 2 million in 1800 to nearly 120 million in 1987. During this period African-Americans constituted a significant proportion of the labor force. The records from 1800 to 1860 show that slave labor constituted 27.4 percent of the labor force in 1800; it peaked in 1810 at 31.7 percent and declined to a low of 21.1 percent in 1860 (U.S. Bureau of the Census, 1975).

Census data from more recent years show that minorities (primarily African-Americans) constituted 11 percent of the U.S. civilian labor force in 1970. The proportion of minorities in the labor force rose significantly to 15.9 percent in 1980 with the addition of Hispanics in the census count: 10.2 percent for African-Americans and 5.7 percent for Hispanics. In 1987 the proportion of minorities increased 2.8 percentage points to constitute 18.7 percent of the labor force. In the year 2000 minorities are projected to constitute 21.9 percent of the labor force: 11.7 percent African-Americans and 10.2 percent Hispanics (U.S. Bureau of the Census, 1989). The rapid increase in minority participation in the work force parallels a significant decline in the proportion of White male workers and portends significant changes for numerous occupations.

Occupational Categories of Minority Employment. In 1987 the U.S.

civilian work force, sixteen years of age and older, consisted of 112,440,000 persons. Of this number, minorities represented 17 percent of the work force: 10.1 percent for African-Americans and 6.9 percent for Hispanics (U.S. Bureau of the Census, 1989). However, of the six broad-based occupational categories monitored by the Bureau of the Census, minorities were not evenly distributed among the various occupations. They tended to be underrepresented among managerial and professional specialists, where they represented 9.9 percent of the employees. They were well represented among technical, sales, and administrative support personnel (14.4 percent), precision production, craft, and repair workers (15.3 percent), and farming, forestry and fishing employees (19.7 percent). And they were overrepresented in service occupations (26.5 percent) and among operators, fabricators, and laborers (26 percent).

Minority Participation in the Emerging Economy. As they respond to the demands of the high-technology revolution, many occupations will undergo substantial transformation. As a consequence these changes could negatively affect the abilities of minority workers to enter and progress in some occupations and may inadvertently seal them into others. However, many observers agree that the emerging economy will have mixed effects on the occupational opportunities and career choices of minorities. For example, Sullivan (1989) conducted research on the occupational absorption rates of African-Americans into African-American-dominated occupations from 1960 to 1980. She concluded that while African-Americans were increasingly being recruited into comparatively integrated occupations, the data did not suggest a decline in the *rate* of desegregation for African-Americans.

Observing that one effect of advanced technology is an increased demand for much higher skill levels for available jobs, Goddard (1989) predicts that by the year 2000 a majority of all new jobs will require a postsecondary education. Several other authors agree and suggest that advanced technology will have the effect of splitting the U.S. occupational structure into two halves: one dominated by upper-level professional service jobs and the other dominated by lower-level maintenance services (food, cleaning, security, and personal). They argue that the middle-range jobs, particularly clerical jobs, will be eliminated by high-technology developments.

By analyzing the occupations with the fastest and largest growth, as well as those that are declining, Sullivan (1989) and Wallace (1989) conclude that minorities will be disproportionately represented in both the new and the old job categories. However, the new jobs in which minorities will *least* likely be found are those closely related to technology (such as electrical and electronics engineers) and management (such as general managers and top executives). They will *most* likely be found in the low-paying, low-technology service jobs that comprise the lower echelon of the service economy (such as nursing aids, orderlies and attendants, janitors and cleaners, truck drivers, and guards). The impact of these changes on the distribution of differentially rewarded positions in the U.S. economy will be increased inequality between the top and the bottom of the occupational distribution.

Goddard (1989) warns that as a result of the occupational transformations stimulated by advanced technology, a new four-tiered working-class system is beginning to take shape in the United States. Ultimately, it is expected to divide workers into four groups: (1) an upper class of professional and managerial workers (25 percent); (2) a middle class of technical, administrative support, and skilled workers (35 percent); (3) a service class of low-technology workers (25 percent); and (4) an underclass of individuals with no steady employment, doing odd jobs and the like (15 percent). The rise of a new low-technology service class and an underclass, both dominated by minorities, could engender class tensions with racial and ethnic overtones.

Human Resource Problems and Issues in Managing Diversity

As an isolated event, the relative increase in minority workers during the 1990s is not problematic. The labor force could simply absorb them into traditional job classifications as it has during the preceding decades. However, when this information is juxtaposed with other trends and perspectives, it becomes abundantly clear that significant and perhaps turbulent changes are in store for most major U.S. industries. Problems and issues will likely arise regarding the workplace training opportunities for minorities, the changing organizational culture and human relationships within the workplace, and the need for remedial programs for individual minorities.

Minority Participation in Workplace Training. Human resources have replaced natural and machine resources as the basic building blocks of production and service (Carnevale, 1989) and now account for more than 80 percent of the nation's total economic output. Therefore, the acquired skills and abilities of workers have become the pivotal resource that drives the U.S economy. Although both pre-employment education and workplace training increase the value of human resources, traditionally they have not been utilized by minorities.

In an analysis of the effects of pre-employment educational attainment and workplace training on employee earnings over a lifetime, Carnevale (1989) argues that only 10 percent of the differences in earnings can be attributed to pre-employment education. Learning on the job accounted for 25 percent of the difference, but the respective amounts of both initial earnings and subsequent formal training received were strongly determined by pre-employment educational attainment. However, once employed, workplace training improved productivity in the present job, earnings on future jobs (by 18 percent over earnings in previous jobs), and durability of effects on earnings (the effects of workplace learning endure thirteen years, compared to eight years for school-based learning).

Although workplace training provides significant advantages in earnings to individual workers, minority workers tend to be tremendously underrepresented among its participants. For example, in 1987 African-American adults constituted 9.5 percent of the work force and Hispanics were 5.5 percent. However, African-Americans received only 5.1 percent of formal workplace training and Hispanics received only 2.7 percent. During this same year, Whites constituted 86 percent of the work force but received 92.2 percent of workplace training (Carnevale, 1989). This observation might be explained in part by the fact that training varies considerably by occupation. Technical and professional employees (among whom minorities tend to be underrepresented) are the most highly trained group, followed by clerical and sales employees. The least educated and trained employees are low-technology service workers (among whom minorities tend to be overrepresented) (Carnevale, 1989).

It appears that the relative position of minorities in the occupational structure tends to inhibit their access to training, that is, employers often do not perceive an adequate cost/benefit to training low-wage entry-level workers, and workers often have low levels of commitment to employers. However, as the labor supply shrinks and global competition increases in intensity, employers will likely engage in quality-improvement efforts to build customer relations throughout the organization (Goddard, 1989). Therefore, they may be required to rethink the strategy of accepting high turnover rates among low-wage entry-level employees and seek to build employee commitment by investing in the long-term benefits of education and training for entry-level workers.

Race Relations and Organizational Culture. The increase in minorities in the workplace will likely coincide with two other emerging trends: increasing reliance on advanced technology and quality-improvement efforts driven by stiff competition in a global marketplace. These two trends are projected to increase the importance of education and skill requirements of individual employees and simultaneously to transform the structure and culture of organizations. Structurally, the hierarchical organizational bureaucracy is expected to succumb to a much more flexible organizational structure characterized by increased reliance on work groups and individual worker autonomy. For example, Goddard (1989) projects that task forces will be organized around problem solving by groups of relative strangers representing a diverse set of professional skills. These groups will evolve in response to problems rather than to programmed role expectations. The manager will be less of a taskmaster and more of a coordinator or linking pin between various task forces. Hierarchical rank and status will not count as much as flexibility and functionality according to education, skill, and professional training.

In a work environment characterized by change and uncertainty, minorities will likely face many challenges to their efforts to maximize their human resource potential and participate as full partners in efforts to achieve the espoused goals of the organization. One of the most significant challenges will likely come not from the structure of the organization but rather from the human relations and political perspectives that define the organization's culture.

In society at-large, minorities and Whites generally live in geographically and socially segregated communities. They often do not encounter each other on a personal level until they either enroll in college or obtain employment. Their perceptions of the other race or ethnic group are likely to be shaped more by the stereotyped images encountered in the broadcast and print media and by the observations of like-race family, friends, and colleagues than by personal experiences. In the past employers could forestall race-related interpersonal conflicts by segregating employees into racially and culturally uniform work groups. However, with the press of advanced technology and quality improvement this strategy is no longer viable.

As minorities increasingly participate in the various levels of the organization and become intimate partners within work groups, their presence will likely increase the amount and intensity of defensive routines experienced within the organizational culture. Most organizations develop defensive routines in order to protect themselves from threat. Defensive routines are any policies or actions that prevent the organization from experiencing pain or threat *and* simultaneously prevent action directed toward correcting the causes of the threat in the first place (Argyris, 1986). One of the most frequent defensive routines is mixed messages. These contain meanings that are simultaneously "ambiguous, and clearly so" and "imprecise, and precisely so" (Argyris, 1986). The recipients of mixed messages experience the dilemmas that the messages are designed to engender.

Mixed messages can be extremely problematic for minority employees. For example, research conducted by Greenhaus, Parasuraman, and Wormley (1990) demonstrated the complex, detrimental effects such messages had on African-American managers. Their research examined the relationships among race, organizational experiences, job performance evaluations, and career outcomes for African-American and White managers from three work organizations. Their research was stimulated by a concern that although African-Americans have gained greater access to managerial jobs, they face "treatment discrimination" in the workplace that can affect job promotions, salary increases, and other aspects of career mobility.

The research surveyed 823 managers (45 percent of whom were African-Americans) and their respective supervisors. The results indicated that race was directly related to the negative job performance evaluations, early career plateauing, and career dissatisfactions reported by African-American managers. Significant race effects were observed in that supervisors were significantly more likely to rate African-Americans lower than Whites on both the relationship and task dimensions of performance. However, the researchers discovered that a portion of the race effects on job performance operated indirectly through the lack of job discretion (that is, decision-making authority) accorded African-American managers and through their lower level of organizational acceptance. The mixed messages were "You are valued by management but not by the organization" and "You were hired because of your competence, but you are not trusted to make important decisions."

Organizational defensive routines organized into self-reinforcing loops can act to create problems such as low performance ratings. They can also act to coerce collusion among human resource professionals to reinforce these conditions (Argyris, 1986). In the future human resource professionals will likely be increasingly challenged to design and implement learning programs to address sensitive and highly emotional race-related issues that are manifested as defensive routines.

Challenges to Workplace Communications. The impending increase of minorities in the workplace will likely increase the number and severity of communication difficulties experienced in many work environments. The likelihood of communication difficulties results from the convergence of two trends: growing literacy demands in the workplace and lower basic-skills levels among employees engaged in many low-technology jobs (Mikulecky, 1990). Also, there are wide racial and ethnic differences in the functional literacy skills of young adults (Kirsch and Jungeblunt, 1986). Although a vast majority of all ethnic populations can accomplish basic literacy tasks, gaps in the populations become wider as the complexity of tasks increases.

Basic literacy refers to the mastery of the oral, cultural, and print communication skills and strategies essential to independent functioning and learning in the workplace. It involves the processes of decoding and of drawing inferences and conclusions from complex material in a wide variety of formats and from different sources. It entails reading, writing, editing, and recognizing patterns in manuals, graphs, computations, correspondence, and print-outs and on CRT screens (Mikulecky, 1990).

Literacy demands in the workplace have increased dramatically over the last two hundred years. During the first decennial census undertaken in 1790, not more than 10 percent of jobs required reading and writing abilities (Mikulecky, 1990). However, Diehl and Mikulecky (1980) found that only 2 percent of the one hundred workers examined from a cross-section of occupations required no reading or writing. Time spent reading texts, charts, graphs, and computer terminals averaged nearly two hours daily. Difficulty levels of 70 percent of the reading materials encountered on the job ranged from ninth- to twelfth-grade levels.

Communication difficulties are particularly important to industry because they can lead to low productivity, lost or damaged material, injuries and even deaths resulting from avoidable accidents, and other problems. For example, productive time may be lost because supervisors must give regular lectures on the use of equipment rather than rely on their employees' ability to use step-by-step written instructions.

As workplace communication difficulties increase, employers will likely invest in workplace literacy programs. These programs are designed to reach academically unskilled employees by offering job-specific instruction using materials and tasks from the workplace. The programs are context-specific, functional, highly focused, and structured for the convenience of the employees. They strongly motivate learners by capitalizing on their familiarity with the subject matter content and providing immediate application of newly learned skills (Nurss and Chase, 1989).

A Typology of Cultural Diversity Program Types

As human resource professionals grapple with the implications of helping managers and employees cope in the new workplace environments created by an influx of minorities, they will likely consider four types of programs (see Figure 1). These programs address the organizational problems created by a culturally diverse work force.

Type 1 programs (indirect/managers) target managers but indirectly address problems and issues related to cultural diversity. For example,

Figure 1. A Typology of Cultural Diversity Programs

	Target Population	
	Managers	Employees
Focus on Cultural Diversity — Indirect	Type 1	Type 2
Focus on Cultural Diversity — Direct	Type 3	Type 4

programs designed to help managers deal with the problems of defensive routines in general can also be useful in solving those problems that specifically originate from mixed messages delivered to minority employees.

Type 2 programs (indirect/employees) target all employees (not just minorities) but indirectly facilitate the resolution of problems and issues that relate to cultural diversity. For example, programs such as Business Writing, Business Math, Manuscript Editing for Professionals, and Oral Communication can be offered directly by the Human Resource Department to all employees but serve in particular to remedy the communication difficulties experienced by some minorities. Other indirect programs could be made available via tuition reimbursement programs that allow employees to take courses from a number of other providers, such as two- and four-year colleges and technical schools.

Type 3 programs (direct/managers) provide instruction to managers in order to directly address organizational problems and issues that result from cultural diversity. For example, training programs could be designed to sensitize supervisors to the reasons for the low performance ratings received by minority managers, or managers could be enrolled in workshops to sensitize them to the work-related cultural perspectives of foreign-born workers.

Type 4 programs (direct/employees) provide instruction to employees in order to directly address organizational concerns that originate with cultural diversity. For example, English as a Second Language classes could be provided for immigrant workers, whether by the human resource department of the organization or through special arrangements with outside sources.

Conclusion

Human resource professionals tend to devote an inordinate amount of attention to the impact of workplace training on the attainment of organizational goals. Although the personal goals of individual workers and the general goals of society are important, they are relevant only to the extent that they are congruent with the goals of the parent organization. From this perspective, the projected influx of significant numbers of minorities into the workplace not only affords human resource managers the opportunity to design and implement innovative programs that contribute substantially to the profitability of the parent organization, but it also provides the opportunity for minorities to improve their personal competencies and for the organization to contribute to the goal of social justice.

References

Argyris, C. "Reinforcing Organizational Defensive Routines: An Unintended Human Resources Activity." *Human Resource Management,* 1986, 25 (4), 541–555.

Carnevale, A. P. "The Learning Enterprise." *Training and Development Journal,* 1989, 43 (2), 26–33.

Copeland, L. "Learning to Manage a Multicultural Work Force." *Training,* May 1988, pp. 49-56.

Diehl, W., and Mikulecky, L. "The Nature of Reading at Work." *Journal of Reading,* 1980, *24,* 221-227.

Goddard, R. W. "Work Force 2000." *Personnel Journal,* 1989, *68* (2), 65-71.

Greenhaus, J. H., Parasuraman, S., and Wormley, W. M. "Effects of Race on Organizational Experiences, Job Performance Evaluations, and Career Outcomes." *Academy of Management Journal,* 1990, *33* (1), 64-86.

Kirsch, I., and Jungeblut, A. *Literacy: Profiles of America's Young Adults, Final Report.* Report no. 16-PL-01. Princeton, N.J.: National Assessment of Educational Progress, 1986.

Mikulecky, L. "Basic Skills Impediments to Communication Between Management and Hourly Employees." *Management Communications Quarterly,* 1990, *3* (4), 452-473.

Nurss, J. R., and Chase, N. D. "Workplace Literacy: A Tool for Recruitment." *Adult Literacy and Basic Education,* 1989, *13* (1), 16-23.

Sullivan, T. A. "Women and Minority Workers in the New Economy: Optimistic, Pessimistic, and Mixed Scenarios." *Work and Occupations,* 1989, *16* (4), 393-415.

U.S. Bureau of the Census. *Historical Statistics of the United States, Colonial Times to 1970.* Part 2. (Bicentennial ed.) Washington, D.C.: Government Printing Office, 1975.

U.S. Bureau of the Census. *Statistical Abstract of the United States: 1989.* (109th ed.) Washington, D.C.: Government Printing Office, 1989.

Wallace, M. "Brave New Workplace: Technology and Work in the New Economy." *Work and Occupations,* 1989, *16* (4), 363-392.

Larry G. Martin is associate professor of adult and continuing education at the University of Wisconsin, Milwaukee.

Jovita M. Ross-Gordon is assistant professor of adult education at The Pennsylvania State University, University Park.

Asian refugees have implemented a model of literacy tailored to their
cultural learning needs and situated in their own neighborhood—
all part of a mainstream vocational-technical institution.

Teaching Their Own: Minority Challenges to Mainstream Institutions

Ronald Podeschi

The often-quoted advice by the philosopher Santayana is that we need to know history so that we do not repeat the mistakes of the past. Another way to make the same point is to emphasize learning from the past by repeating its successes. The history of the United States includes ethnic groups successfully educating their own people when mainstream institutions made the mistake of neglecting the cultural backgrounds of their students. This chapter explores this history, probes pertinent perspectives on culture, and describes how and why Southeast Asian refugees recently implemented a new model of an old idea: teaching their own adults.

We in the field of adult education in the late twentieth century need to realize that minority challenges to educational mainstream institutions are not new or uncommon. In the late nineteenth and early twentieth centuries, German immigrants fought for bilingual instruction in public schools, Polish immigrants sought protection against Americanization by establishing parochial schools, while other European immigrants in various ways and degrees tried to maintain their respective cultural identities and resist the domination of their children by mainstream values. Adult education in the United States has its parallel history, especially since most European immigrants were adults at the time of their arrival. Seller (1978) points out that over two-and-one-half million of the almost three million non-English-speaking immigrants in 1910 were over twenty years old.

The mainstream response to the educational needs of the exploding adult immigrant population early in this century came primarily through the night school, with a declared emphasis on learning English. However, as Seller (1978) points out, training in virtues of citizenship and work habits were aimed at men, while women received lessons in hygiene, child care, and homemaking. By the early 1920s, less than 2 percent of the fourteen million non-naturalized immigrants actually attended night school. Seller explains what happened: "Immigrant communities succeeded where American educators failed because they provided education planned and executed by immigrants themselves, or by second generation members of the ethnic communities; they taught in immigrant languages and in ways that did not violate immigrant cultural traditions; and classes were located in and sponsored by institutions immigrants knew and trusted—the lodge, the church, the union" (1978, p. 88).

These trusted educational programs helped fulfill two kinds of freedom important to the new immigrants (Smith, 1969). Freedom in the New World meant opportunity for personal advancement after leaving the Old World, where it was not possible. Second, American freedom meant the liberty to maintain the cultural life of their own ethnic group.

However, cultural pluralism and assimilation have always been in tension in the history of this nation. The history of the night schools in New York City demonstrates the national experience. Berrol (1976, p. 210) points out that the explosion of night schools "was in direct response to the immigrant 'invasion' because, to many New Yorkers of seventy years ago, the hordes of Italians, Slavs, and Eastern European Jews who poured into the city were alarmingly foreign and needed to be assimilated into the mainstream as soon as possible." Although explaining that poor attendance was affected by various program and staff deficiencies, she emphasizes that the gap between enrollment and attendance led to increasing recognition that many of the immigrants did not want to give up their own cultures.

Cultural Perspectives

In the last decade of the twentieth century, culture is still a key in effective evaluation of those whose lives are not part of mainstream society. To emphasize the importance of cultural values, though, does not imply that all members from a minority group share the same cultural meanings. As Eisenhart (1989) makes clear, culture is context-dependent and emergent.

For adults who are struggling at basic literacy levels, and who have little or no experience in successful formal education, cultural influence from their own ethnic group carries even more force. For this reason, and on the basis of empirical studies, Reder (1985) strongly advocates literacy training in adults' own settings. "Learners need not feel (as they often do) that becoming more literate means abandoning friends, families, and peer values to join a larger, more impersonal world dominated by alien and sometimes hostile institutions and values" (1985, p. 2). Pointing to school research, Reder concludes that "lower track" students can be reached by utilizing materials common in the daily life of the community. He suggests that this strategy can best be applied to adults by utilizing existing community networks and teachers who are of the same background as the learners.

Institutions (like schools), as well as individuals, have cultural habits: they carry value beliefs in what they consider good and right. When individuals from minority backgrounds face conflicting values in mainstream institutions, alienation can result. In educational institutions, even with commitment and good intentions from mainstream staff, teaching and learning environments can be dominated in subtle but powerful ways by mainstream value assumptions.

A leading example of a source of potential tension for minority learners in educational institutions is the mainstream value of *individualism*. As analyzed elsewhere (Podeschi, 1986), this core value in the United States emphasizes independence through individual achievement, self-motivation, and self-reliance—significantly affecting theory and practice in adult education. Such an emphasis contrasts with the value of *interdependence* that stresses collective achievement and collective responsibility.

As Pratt (1988, p. 356) contends, "the psychological perspectives which dominate adult education literature in North America are stridently individualistic, presenting learning as a change in individual behavior, cognition, or predisposition but always within the ethos of the dominant individualistic culture of the United States." His study of Canadian Indians shows contrasting learning processes that are collective in character and where the worth of the learning is not rooted in individual pursuits. And in analyzing American Indian teaching processes, Marashio (1982) lays out inherent connections between Indian oral and spiritual traditions and the collective value of wisdom, knowledge, and skills.

The individual/collective distinction in values may be pertinent to the education of all minority groups to some degree. The importance of interdependence in contrast to individualism, at least in the concept of the extended family, can be seen as well in Hispanics, African-Americans, Asians and other groups whose traditional cultural values are different from the mainstream.

The potential effects of a collective emphasis on learning can be seen vividly in Hvitfeldt's (1986) study of the classroom behavior of Hmong adults. She concludes that these Southeast Asian refugees emphasize "cooperative achievement, the denial of individual ability, and the belief that everyone's classroom work belongs to everyone else" (1986, p. 72). Her study also demonstrates how other cultural values may affect minority adult learning. Hmong adults show a need for explicit teacher direction, paralleling Hmong reliance on authority and leadership. Hvitfeldt (1986, p. 75) explains, "In all areas of social life, Hmong adults exhibit a preference for structure which is imposed from the outside over that which must be individually constructed."

Such Hmong learning needs and preferences can be contrasted with current emphases on teacher-student equality and self-directed learning in humanistic adult education, as analyzed by Elias and Merriam (1980). At the same time, Hmong learning style can be contrasted in some ways with another mainstream philosophy in American adult education, the behaviorist approach, which emphasizes efficiency, measurability, and competencies cut up and categorized. The Hmong, according to Hvitfeldt, have a holistic rather than an analytic perceptual style in their interaction with classroom materials, attending to the whole rather than to the part, focusing on meaning rather than category, and using methods of concept formation based on their own experiences.

The central argument of this chapter, in favor of minorities teaching their own, is that potential conflicts and their effects from contrasting cultural patterns on teaching and learning will be diminished if the instructors are from the same cultural backgrounds as the students. This does not mean that culturally sensitive and knowledgeable instructors from other backgrounds are unable to be effective. Rather, cultural value compatibility is being emphasized here because mainstream practices in adult education can be so ingrained in institutional life that there is little staff awareness of possible value conflict between staff and students.

In addition to such minority involvement in teaching their own, genuine empowerment of minority groups also means involvement in the institutional processes necessary for putting in place teachers from their own groups. Next, we look into a recent example of such empowerment of a new minority in Wisconsin, a state whose history is steeped with European immigrants adapting to a new society.

Case Study of Southeast Asian Refugees

The Hmong in Milwaukee number near six thousand, about one-third of the Hmong in Wisconsin, which is second only to California in Hmong population. Escaping from the rural mountains of Laos because they fought for the United States in the Vietnam War, these pretechnological refugees face survival in a metropolitan city in the most technologically oriented nation in the world. Although culturally from an oral tradition, with little or no formal schooling, the Hmong realize that education is a key to their survival. Whereas the younger Hmong have the opportunity to acquire mainstream language and skills, the adults face much steeper mountains in gaining access to jobs, support services, and day-to-day security in the land of bureaucratic individualism.

The Problem and Its Context. The vocational-technical educational system in the Milwaukee area is nationally known for its various programs serving a diverse student population. The central city campus is the largest and most visible educational institution at present for minority adults, including the recent Southeast Asian refugees. Although striving to serve inner-city students, and although ahead of other postsecondary institutions in serving Asian refugees, this vocational-technical campus struggled during the 1980s to meet the needs of the Hmong. At least this is how the Hmong leadership saw the situation by the end of the decade.

The results of a questionnaire survey conducted by the refugee leadership confirmed their perceptions. The responses from seventy-nine refugee adults attending English as a Second Language (ESL) and vocational classes at the local campus troubled their leadership. Two-thirds of the respondents said that they experienced "great difficulty" understanding their instructors, one-half of the students "did not understand what they were studying in class," and most felt that help must come from someone who could speak their language. Besides language barriers, the students found it difficult to adjust to the Americanized teaching methods that ignored their cultural learning patterns.

In addition to traditional value patterns, an individual's culture also includes socioeconomic dimensions. In ESL classes, the Hmong found themselves with classmates from around the world who came to the United States with a background of formal education and related skills. In contrast, as shown by an examination of the educational levels of a sample of three hundred Hmong receiving supportive services at their self-help organization, the average education in Laos of these refugees is only two years. For these learners, not having the same general background of literacy as other students in their classes, self-esteem is even more problematic.

Although the general educational problems of Hmong adults parallel those of other minorities, past and present, solutions to such problems need to be probed in the specific context in which a particular group finds itself. Whereas the Hmong refugees in some smaller Wisconsin cities confront mainstream institutions that have no experience with a linguistic and cultural minority, a different problem exists for them in a metropolitan city with diverse populations. In the city, they are competing with other minority groups—groups with more experience and clout—for attention and resources. For example, although adult bilingual classes were being taught in Milwaukee, even in community settings, the Hmong found themselves confronting an institutional mind-set that equated bilingual classes with Spanish-speaking students.

The Solution and Its Context. In order to obtain funding from the vocational-technical institution for bilingual literacy classes to be taught by a Hmong in their own neighborhood, the Hmong leadership sought out the one administrator who could most help them, an Hispanic dean who believes strongly in community-based bilingual education. They knew that they needed a key administrator with decision-making power in the educational bureaucracy, especially since the ESL Department maintained a teaching philosophy of English-only. Within weeks, with funding set, the

Hmong recruited from out of state one of their own who had the credentials to be the full-time instructor, and they worked out a classroom area in the building that houses their self-help organization. With an additional part-time instructor, the program began in March 1989, with an enrollment of over fifty adult learners at the lowest levels of literacy.

After the first year of the program, and the addition of another Hmong part-time instructor, enrollment is now up to over ninety students, with over 90-percent attendance and 80-percent continuation rates. The 20-percent dropout rate is affected by family moves from Milwaukee, health problems, and conflicts with jobs or child rearing. Ages of the students range from eighteen to seventy-five, with two-thirds being women.

The feedback to the head instructor from students who had experienced instruction in mainstream settings points to a key difference in this program: The students are better able to connect their learning to their own experience. They feel that they learn more, are less stressed, are treated with more respect, and are more comfortable being with other Hmong. Whereas they see class time going quickly here, time moved slowly in their earlier classes and they "could not wait to get home."

Besides knowing the students well in terms of their cultural traditions, the instructor understands them in the context of their refugee experience, having gone through it himself with his family. He is careful not to hurt their emotions and their self-concepts. Whereas shyness is typical of Hmong in mainstream classes, here they are not embarrassed because "we are all in the same boat." And the instructor enhances their security, especially those who are older, with such statements as "Do not feel lower than me, think of me as your son or your brother. I know that you are respected members of your family because of your experience and wisdom."

At the same time, the instructor knows that as a Hmong he has strong respect as a teacher, and he maintains a formal relationship, making his expectations clear to the students. Yet, it is a personalized relationship, one of mutual respect. Knowing the Hmong cultural emphasis on collective responsibility, he works them as a whole, encouraging cooperation. But he realizes that the women, given the cultural gender patterns, may be reticent in front of men, or that men may be embarrassed by not being able to keep up with women. As a group, they become aware of their cultural dilemmas, and they laugh together.

Utilizing his knowledge of the Hmong language, the instructor is able to make learning connections for the students. For example, it is explained that the letter j is pronounced in English as the word fish is pronounced in Hmong. And instead of breaking up an English word from left to right as a linear Westerner would do, the instructor uses Hmong holistic perception and starts at the rightmost end of the word. Although many are unable to read and write in their own language as well as in English, the students learn from their instructor that they do have a "literacy" of their own. Such literacy can be not only in the Hmong language but also in the form of their traditional artwork—at which Hmong women excel—and the instructor uses this literacy as a base for them to learn written English.

Although teaching them as a group, he individualizes the students' experiences and their progress in the class. The students become less dependent on him as they gain confidence as learners. Assessing their folders of written work, tests, and class work, the instructor accordingly changes the English and math content level for the group. At the end of the semester, some students move up to the next class level and do so with Hmong quiet pride. When the three classes come together for a party at the end of the semester, those in the highest level feel at the top of the school, even though they are only at about a fourth-grade level of English and math literacy.

The Model's Assumptions. In looking at this program from the outside, we can try to ascertain its underlying philosophy. It is less difficult to say what it is not. It is not either of the two primary models of literacy programming described in a recent symposium at an adult education research conference (Hiemstra and others, 1986). This Hmong program contradicts some of the basic assumptions of the dominant model in the United States (individual-oriented literacy programs), in which illiteracy is perceived as an individual deficit in attitude as well as cognition, and in which there is a belief that illiteracy can be remedied with standardized instruction and uniform materials. So too, the Hmong program contradicts some of the basic assumptions of the model now emerging in the United States (community-based literacy programs), in which the curriculum is shaped toward political change, and in which there is no funding from mainstream sources.

Although contradicting some assumptions of these other two models, the Hmong program does share other assumptions of each of the models. It parallels, for example, the individual-oriented model by having a mission that is focused on skill development, one that is politically nonthreatening and that gains stable funding. On the other side, it parallels the community-based model by having a definable constituency, one that is not reached by other programs.

This "in-between" position of the Hmong program reflects their approach to change. As Dunnigan (1986) explains in his anthropological history of Hmong adaptation, the Hmong see accommodation and compromise as more effective than direct confrontation in accomplishing goals. They have developed a survival approach that maintains a cultural independence, on the one hand, and an ability to enlist the cooperation of mainstream resources, on the other. Although their approach may not be suitable for other minority groups, this synthesis of independence and cooperation works for them.

The instructional approach of this program also points to an "in-between" position, one between a formal training program and informal literacy networks. Recent ethnographic studies, according to Reder (1985), show the "natural" way in which literacy skills can be socialized outside of formal programs. Utilizing the term "scaffolding" to describe means of providing auxiliary support to learners as they seek to accomplish the tasks set by the teacher, Reder points out that the trust and rapport in natural or informal literacy networks can provide effective contexts for the introduction of scaffolding into the formal education of adults.

This integration of natural networks and formal instruction works both ways in the Hmong program. An instructional approach that draws on the literacy tasks and activities in which the learners are meaningfully involved in informal settings can enhance the formal training. But also a community-based class can help lead those who are isolated from viable networks (for example, Hmong elderly, young mothers) into settings in which they become part of new helping networks inside and outside of class.

The connection between classroom learning for "low level" adults and outside uses of literacy is apparent in the workplace environment. In a review of research on adult literacy education, Sticht (1988–1989, pp. 70–71) concludes that "the social nature of the uses of literacy may account, at least in part, for why many of those with low literacy skills as assessed by standardized tests may, in fact, perform quite well in settings in which the literacy demands for task accomplishment would seem to ensure failure." A case in point is the Hmong in Milwaukee, who are increasingly obtaining and retaining jobs partly because they often work in a group, in which one of them is bilingual and becomes the liaison and teacher for the rest.

This connection between the day-to-day world of survival and formal instruction is one reason that the head teacher in the Hmong literacy program would like to expand the classes to include training in areas such as drivers' licenses, government regulations, and even child rearing. Such classes will be enhanced if materials are developed that integrate bilingual literacy instruction with the skills training needed for adaptation to the new society.

One enhancement of the connection between day-to-day life and literacy training will be a new Hmong day-care center for the children of those in classes. Housed close to the instructional site, the center will attend to one of the problems that became apparent early in the program: The Hmong, who tend to have several children, started bringing them to class. For the instructors, this practice involved too much integration between formal education and the students' social worlds. Again, cooperating with a mainstream institution, this time with the public school system, the Hmong are now receiving funding for the day-care center. As their children are cared for, the parents can be learners in the literacy classes. And as they gain literacy skills, they can become teachers of their preschool children who are being readied for formal learning.

Summary

Looking back at this model, what are its primary ingredients? There are seven: (1) The basic assumptions of the literacy program and site are consistent with the cultural assumptions of the specific minority group it is serving. (2) The instructors are of the same cultural background as the students, which gives them bases of shared experiential knowledge, trust, and security. (3) The teaching processes match the learning assumptions of the cultural group. (4) There is a natural integration between formal instruction and informal social networks. (5) There are viable connections between classroom learning and outside uses of literacy. (6) Significant social needs of the students (such as day care) are given attention by the literacy program. (7) The change strategies utilized in bringing about the literacy program are consistent with the cultural assumptions of the specific minority group.

No matter what minority group, or whether adults or children, in the United States they all face a rapidly changing technological society in which education and skills are necessary. One significant difference between current racial and ethnic minorities and the earlier European immigrants is that the nation a century ago was expanding with industrialization; it was a time when school dropouts totaled 90 percent and there was little national concern. Adult literacy education, as Sticht (1988-1989) explains, was not seen as a national social problem; there were but a few scattered efforts, little development of curriculum material, and poor methods based on schooling practices. Today, the national concern about the education of minorities is at a peak, due mainly to demographic predictions and employment needs for the twenty-first century.

Whether we can learn from our history will be seen in coming years. We may need to remind ourselves that our history of groups who successfully "teach their own" does not pertain to just White immigrants. The past century is filled with statistics and stories of African-American institutions of higher education (Hill, 1985; Naipaul, 1989). And there are numerous examples in the adult education literature of African-Americans teaching their own early in this century (Briscoe and Ross, 1989; Neverdon-Morton, 1982; De Vaughan, 1986).

However, we must remember such racial minority developments took place in contexts of societal racism and powerlessness. Most current minorities are part of what Ogbu (1978) sees as "historical, structural" minorities—groups who have survived extreme legal, social, economic, and political restrictions. The challenges to mainstream institutions at the end of the twentieth century to bring about programs of minorities teaching their own, building upon the successes without the mistakes in our history, involve struggles that can benefit from the participation of the descendants of European immigrants as well as the leadership of racial minorities.

References

Berrol, S. "From Compensatory Education to Adult Education: The New York City Evening Schools, 1825-1935." *Adult Education,* 1976, *26* (4), 208-225.

Briscoe, D. B., and Ross, J. M. "Racial and Ethnic Minorities and Adult Education." In S. B. Merriam and P. M. Cunningham (eds.), *Handbook of Adult and Continuing Education.* San Francisco: Jossey-Bass, 1989.

De Vaughan, B. T. "The Boston Literary Society and Historical Association: An Early 20th Century Example of Adult Education as Conducted by a Black Voluntary Association." *Lifelong Learning,* 1986, *9* (4), 11-12, 16.

Dunnigan, T. "Processes of Identity Maintenance in Hmong Society." In G. Hendricks, B. Downing, and A. Deinard (eds.), *The Hmong in Transition.* Staten Island, N.Y.: Center for Migration Studies, 1986.

Eisenhart, M. "Reconsidering Cultural Differences in American Schools." *Educational Foundations,* 1989, *3* (2), 51-68.

Elias, J., and Merriam, S. B. *Philosophical Foundations of Adult Education.* Huntington, N.Y.: Krieger, 1980.

Hiemstra, R., and others. "The Ends and Means of Adult Literacy Education." In *Proceedings of the Twenty-Seventh Annual Meeting of the Adult Education Research Conference.* Syracuse, N.Y.: Syracuse University, 1986.

Hill, S. *The Traditionally Black Institutions of Higher Education, 1860-1982.* Office of Educational Research and Improvement and the National Center for Education Statistics. Washington, D.C.: Government Printing Office, 1985. (ED 1.102 B56)

Hvitfeldt, C. "Traditional Culture, Perceptual Style, and Learning: The Classroom Behavior of Hmong Adults." *Adult Education Quarterly,* 1986, *36* (2), 65-77.

Marashio, P. "Enlighten My Mind . . . Examining the Learning Process Through Native Americans' Ways." *Journal of American Indian Education,* Feb. 1982, pp. 2-10.

Naipaul, V. S. *A Turn in the South.* New York: Knopf, 1989.

Neverdon-Morton, C. "Self-Help Programs as Educative Activity of Black Women in the South, 1895-1925: Focus on Four Key Areas." *Journal of Negro Education,* 1982, *51* (3), 207-220.

Ogbu, J. *Minority Education and Caste: The American System in Cross-Cultural Perspective.* Orlando, Fla.: Academic Press, 1978.

Podeschi, R. "Philosophies, Practices, and American Values." *Lifelong Learning,* 1986, *9* (4), 4-6, 27-28.

Pratt, P. "Cross-Cultural Relevance of Selected Psychological Perspectives on Learning." In M. Zukas (ed.), *Proceedings of Transatlantic Dialogue: A Research Exchange.* Leeds, England: University of Leeds, 1988.

Reder, S. *Giving Literacy Away: Alternative Strategies for Increasing Adult Literacy Development.* Washington, D.C.: National Institute of Education, 1985. (ED 253 775)

Seller, M. "Success and Failure in Adult Education: The Immigrant Experience, 1914-1924." *Adult Education,* 1978, *28* (2), 83-99.

Smith, T. "Immigrant Social Aspirations and American Education, 1880-1930." *American Quarterly,* 1969, *21* (3-4), 523-543.

Sticht, T. "Adult Literacy Education." In E. Rothkopf (ed.), *Review of Research in Education.* Vol. 15. Washington, D.C.: American Educational Research Association, 1988-1989.

Ronald Podeschi is professor of educational policy and community studies at the University of Wisconsin, Milwaukee. During the last decade, he has worked closely with Hmong leaders as well as taught courses on and researched refugee adaptation.

Educators and policymakers have been slow to recognize that involving low-income minority parents in the educational process is an asset rather than a liability.

The Changing Role of Low-Income Minority Parents in Their Children's Schooling

Frank E. Nardine

The overarching concept of any discussion of parent-child relationships is the idea that parents play a significant role in the rearing of their children. During the child's formative years and later, parents transmit values, understandings, and skills that are critical in the development of the child's learning process. A common saying refers to the parent as the child's first and most influential teacher. An expectation prevails in our society that children should have knowledgeable and responsible parents who are interested in their children's education and actively participate in it. That is, parents ought to be involved. Cavazos (1985, p. 1) describes parent involvement as "a relationship between families and schools in which parents and educators work together to provide the best possible environment for the schooling of children." The literature on parental involvement is similar to the child development literature inasmuch as it generally tends to emphasize parental influence on children. A more accurate account of parent-child interaction suggests that the relationship is reciprocal. That is, parent and child each influence the other. Only recently has this reciprocal relationship been viewed as a critical factor in adult learning.

The following discussion examines ways in which low-income, culturally unique parents historically have become involved in the educational process of their children. Then, a unique after-school computer education program involving inner-city parents of school-age children is described, which offers some insight into parent-child/child-parent influence. This

NEW DIRECTIONS FOR ADULT AND CONTINUING EDUCATION, no. 48, Winter 1990 © Jossey-Bass Inc., Publishers program exemplifies a novel intergenerational approach to how a child's learning success involves parents and affects them as adult learners.

Role of Tradition in School Involvement

It is not unusual for educators to berate parents for not attending parent-teacher conferences and school events and to accuse them of not being interested in their children's education. In accounting for this parental behavior, the role that cultural tradition and experience play is often overlooked. While it may be true that the increasing demands on all parents in contemporary society dictate that most parents need to be more involved in the schooling of their children, the primary target for increased parental involvement has been low-income parents. As Moles (1987) reports, a survey of low-income parents (earning under $7,000 a year) showed that only 24 percent had two or more contacts with schools in the two years preceding. In the same survey, those parents who had multiple school contacts were "women, whites, higher-income persons, and college-educated" (1987, p. 138). It appears that on the average middle- and upper-class parents traditionally have been involved in the schooling of their children on a regular basis. As a consequence teachers and school administrators have been relatively more open and responsive to their requests and visits. Also these parents (especially the mothers) have been more active in parent-teacher organizations, less reluctant to attend school board meetings and express their views and concerns, and more apt to intervene for their children when they deem that some situation needs their attention. In contrast, there is not a comparable tradition for less-advantaged parents. Access to school administrators and teachers oftentimes is not as easy to obtain, and the importance of joining and participating in school organizations has not been fully realized. Instances of expressing their views and concerns about school and insisting that certain courses of action be taken for their children have been the exception rather than the rule. Low-income, minority parents consequently have not become involved in their children's schooling to a degree comparable to the involvement of middle- and upper-class parents. Why this is true may not be fully understood and appreciated by administrators, teachers, or even the parents themselves.

Deficit Model and Early Parent Education

Historically, the rearing and educating of children were viewed and practiced as quite distinct activities: parents reared, teachers educated. While a comprehensive history of parent education has not yet been written, a summary by Schlossman (1976) provides an informative overview. Parent education itself probably came into existence when teachers, clergy, and others perceived defects in child-rearing practices of parents. The first institution for remedying the defects was colonial America's Sunday school. Impoverished homes were not seen as providing adequate supervision and moral training. In addition to religious instruction, Sunday school teachers communicated what was considered acceptable social behavior and attitudes to their charges who, in turn, transmitted them to their parents. Instead of trying to educate the parents directly, this instruction served as surrogate or compensatory parenting. Gradually intervention and instruction in acceptable child-rearing practices became commonplace. In effect, however, there was a stigma attached to this early kind of parent education. The recipients were viewed as deficient in important aspects of parenting skills.

Following the colonial period, a related parent education approach evolved for immigrant adults who were settling in America in considerable numbers. Tyack (1974) reports that foreign parents, in having different languages, customs, and values, posed a threat to the status quo. Instruction in parent education was used to "acculturate" them into the established and accepted American way of life. Parent education served as an effective vehicle to reduce or eliminate cultural diversity. It was seen as a necessity because authorities continued to have little respect for and faith in the child-rearing practices of lower-class parents and the newly arrived.

The late nineteenth and early twentieth centuries brought a massive wave of European immigrants. Assimilation of the children of these often-poor families into the existing educational system was a daunting task. Parent education burgeoned during this time (Schlossman, 1976). PTAs utilized the strategies of group instruction, home instruction for the poor, and local social-political action in order to reach parents. Home instruction for the poor was formulated by middle-class mothers from their perspective, and more likely as not it was a kind of benign cultural imposition providing clear-cut child-rearing "do's" and "don't's." Schlossman argues that during the decade of the 1920s parent education programs and instruction lost contact with the poor and became a kind of middle-class obsession. Nursery schools were founded to demonstrate to middle-class parents how to raise "children who were deferential to authority, in total control of their emotions, and socially conformist" (1976, p. 457). Even though this period was characterized by the acceptance of and need for parent education (that is, expert guidance about the nature and nurture of their children), the existence of nursery schools removed children from mothers' exclusive control in order to instill acceptable and correct behavior in them. Implicit in the nursery school curriculum was the goal of overcoming deficient middle-class child-rearing practices—not unlike the deficit model approach mentioned previously.

What followed in the succeeding decades was a dramatic shift in how the family was perceived. A depression followed by a major war, coupled with changing cultural values, exposed the vulnerability or dependency of many families, especially those at the lower end of the socioeconomic continuum. The state of American society seriously challenged the notion of the family as self-sufficient. The living and working conditions that beset impoverished families were seen by policymakers and educators to hinder youngsters in school achievement and success in later life. Improvement was thought to be possible only with massive outside assistance. The programs created were intended to combat societally imposed deficits and provide the foundation for individual autonomy. Federal funds and efforts were directed toward early childhood intervention programs concerned with the total development of the child.

Educational intervention with accompanying compensatory experiences, mainly provided by outside sources, was an attempt to overcome deficits derived from home limitations. The launching of Project Headstart exemplified this approach. Impoverished parents were once again seen as lacking in child-rearing and educational skills, which resulted in children beginning school with significant educational and social deficiencies.

Concept of Empowerment

In the 1950s and 1960s educators and policymakers continued to view low-income parents (increasingly single, minority mothers) as not possessing the necessary knowledge and skills to raise children correctly or efficiently. In effect, a deficit model was again applied to the ways in which low-income and minority parents were raising their children. The notion of compensatory education underscored the perceived need for outside resources to overcome the substandard care and restricted educational experiences of the home environment. Cohen (1968) attributed a continuation of racial inequality in educational opportunity to the compensatory education concept. In an insightful analysis of these preschool programs, Bronfenbrenner (1974) documents how this deficit model approach may have undermined the role and status of the parent and consequently affected youngsters' achievement.

The issue of inequality of educational opportunity may have been a contributing factor to the awareness that social barriers contributed immensely to noninvolvement in the educational process by low-income parents. In effect, disadvantaged parents and their children had suffered a tradition of educational disenfranchisement. The research findings of James Coleman (1966) awakened the American conscience in terms of equal rights and equal opportunity for African-Americans and other minority groups. The report "Reconnection for Learning: A Community School System for New York City" (Mayor's Advisory Panel . . . , 1967) advocated not only a redistribution of power but also a new means of energizing school reform through the active inclusion of parents and the community-at-large in the educational process. Fantini (1968) furthered the cause of parental involvement by criticizing the schools as discounting the consumers' preference. He maintained there was no feedback loop from parents or pupils, and "lacking feedback, the system is not likely to respond to changing conditions or needs" (1968, p. 173). He suggested that real parental participation will engender responsibility for what happens in the school, and that the consumers will feel ownership and be likely to pay close attention to actual performance. Finally, he argued that by encouraging active parental participation in the schools' educational process, this experience would provide new insights and knowledge leading to improved child-rearing practices in the home.

With this beginning in the 1960s, educational policymakers began to look to parental involvement as a promising way to improve educational outcomes for poor or underachieving students. Slightly more than ten years ago, the Education Commission of the States published *Families and Schools: Implementing Parent Education*. In this publication Hughes (1979) argued that the term "parent education" was too restrictive and narrow. The focus, he maintained, should be on the family and the interaction of family members, especially between child and parent. Whereas parent education traditionally emphasized early childhood and primary grade levels, Hughes advocated a much broader definition of parental involvement, encompassing family-child and family-school interaction.

Urie Bronfenbrenner and Moncrief Cochran studied the family and took exception to the deficit model attributed to low-income, disadvantaged parents. One of their primary assumptions was that all families have some strengths. They viewed less-advantaged parents as competent rather than incompetent. They attributed most of the poor environmental conditions that beset poor families to sources beyond their control. Although they did not invent the term, their focus and research in the 1970s contributed greatly to the concept of empowerment. Cochran (1987) traces the evolution of the concept of empowerment and defines the term as an interactive process between people and controlling institutions. Through mutual respect and critical reflection, changes occur by which people gain greater influence over the elements in society that restrict their efforts to achieve equal status for themselves and others.

Cochran's definition is reminiscent of Fantini's because it implies a redistribution of power from the have's to the have-not's. Cochran and Henderson (1986) report the results of a two-year study that attempted to empower urban families by providing a variety of support systems to parents and other adults directly involved in the care, upbringing, and education of urban youngsters. During a complicated process of home visits with parents and their children, the parents were viewed in word and deed as experts about their own children. Early home visits were spent in "learning about the parents' views of the child and seeking out examples of activities that were already being carried out with the child and defined by the parent as important to the child's development" (1986, p. 15). By design, this approach recognized the importance of the parenting role, reinforced and enriched ongoing parent-child activities, and encouraged parents to share their knowledge about child care and community services with other parents. The overall strategy involved valuing the parent.

Cochran and Henderson (1986) report that a number of key findings resulted from the study known as the Family Matters Program. Specifically, mothers' feelings about themselves improved (more pronounced for single mothers), parental relations with relatives and friends improved, and contacts with the schools increased, but only in those instances when the child was perceived as having school-related difficulty. The program appears to have been successful at interacting positively with families and influencing specific attitudes and behaviors. But as Cochran (1982, p. 20) reports, "the program was only partially able to stimulate peer interaction and critical reflection, and failed to address the question of changing the balance of power between families and controlling institutions."

Current Status of Parental Involvement and Education

Henderson (1987) provides a comprehensive review of forty-nine studies about the effects of parental involvement. In her summary she concludes that the creation of a positive learning environment at home, including the encouragement of positive attitudes toward education and high expectations of children's success, has a powerful impact on student achievement. Many of the studies reviewed focused on at-risk students. At-risk generally is ascribed to those youngsters who, without intervention of some kind, will be failures or noncontributing adult citizens (Wilensky and Kline, 1988). More often than not they live in households headed by a female parent of low socioeconomic status, where chronic poverty prevails. Unemployment is the rule, but if the mother is employed, the job involves low-level skills for which she is underpaid. The impact of environmental deficits on children appears to impair overall intellectual, psychological, and social skills development. Henderson (1987) concludes, nevertheless, that at-risk younger children outperform their peers if parents are given training in home-teaching techniques. Elementary and middle school learners respond to home-based encouragement where parents both expect and recognize school success. It appears, she concludes, that whenever "parents show an interest in their children's education and set high expectations for their performance, they are promoting attitudes that are keys to achievement, attitudes that can be formed independently of social class or other external circumstances" (1987, p. 4). Henderson (1988) also reports that parental involvement, while important, is not a panacea. Although at-risk youngsters outperform their peers if parents are given training in home-teaching techniques, their achievements still tend to be below average in academic areas.

A review of the literature reveals a paucity of studies that deal with the challenge of finding ways to build and sustain parental involvement in communities composed of low-income, minority parents. The scholars who have addressed this concern emphasize that the development of sound parental involvement programs within these communities would take an extended period of time.

Comer (1988, 1989) has described a parental involvement program initially begun in two inner-city schools in New Haven, Connecticut. He indicates that, at the outset, anger, apathy, and even conflict typified the interaction among parents, school personnel, and pupils. Comer maintains that parental behavior is partly conditioned by inexperience and undereducation, which prohibit positive participation in an organization as complex as a school. As a result of these factors, a great deal of home-school distrust and alienation was evident. Comer and his staff analyzed the situation and ascribed the behavior of minority parents and their children to "sociocultural-misalignment" problems resulting from their status outside society's mainstream. In contrast to a child whose development and experiences coincide with the mainstream values prevalent at school, a youngster from a poor, marginal family more likely than not enters school inadequately prepared. If language skills, reading habits, and social development are underdeveloped or nonstandard, then the youngster can not easily fit into and learn from the mainstream school experience. Comer's solution was the fostering of positive interaction between parents and school personnel on a formal and social level. A management and governance team composed of elected parents and teachers, a mental health specialist, and a member of the nonprofessional support staff was created. Headed by the school principal, the team discussed and solved professional and social problems by group consensus. Key ingredients included communication, interaction, and mutual respect. Parents were invited to become involved, to participate actively, and to help formulate school policy and programs. Comer reports that a key element in the program's success was helping principals to understand and accept a different management style. By sharing administrative power, their ability to manage was increased. School climate and student behavior improved and parental involvement in school affairs increased.

Lightfoot (1978) provides perhaps the most explicit description of the interaction between parent and teacher in attempts to build a home-school connection. Because each has specific role responsibilities—the parent viewing the child as an individual and the teacher viewing the child as a group member—conflict is inevitable due to role differentiation. According to Lightfoot, rather than blame or excuse low-income, minority parents for any intellectual, social, and psychological deficits that their children may possess, educators need to develop adaptive strategies for dealing with these parents. Adaptive strategies negate the demand that parents adjust to meet the school's agenda.

McLaughlin and Shields (1987) maintain, however, that most schools and school systems do not have appropriate structures and appropriate strategies that would permit low-income parents to become meaningfully involved. What exist are models of parental involvement developed by and aimed at "parents in the mainstream." In addressing the role of policy in nurturing meaningful parental involvement, these authors conclude that "effective parent-involvement strategies hinge on local realities and on the attitudes and beliefs of those individuals . . . who are primarily responsible for the implementation of such strategies" (1987, p. 158). McLaughlin and Shields advocate that educators and others must change beliefs and attitudes they hold about low-income or poorly educated parents if meaningful parental involvement is to result. They advocate policy and administrative practices based on a combination of pressure and support that serves to encourage administrators and teachers to adopt innovative parental involvement activities. Critical in the process are incentives. Incentives include information about successful programs, small grants, or other reinforcers to motivate educators to try new practices, expectation and recognition of professional behavior that initiates parental involvement activities, and leadership by administrative and organizational personnel that advocates parental involvement. Only through these and other incentives will educators realize that parental involvement is an important, if not essential, element in educating at-risk youngsters. This insight, according to McLaughlin and Shields, will serve as a positive influence on educators to modify their attitudes regarding the role that low-income parents can play in their children's education.

Getting to Parents Through Their Children

The program described below involves a youth club located in the inner-city of a large metropolitan area in the Midwest. The program consists of club members and their parents and centers on teaching computer skills to at-risk pupils. The capabilities of the personal computer are viewed as extremely well suited for aiding at-risk youngsters in overcoming many of the learning difficulties encountered in school (Bialo and Sivin, 1989). Unfortunately, the nearby all-Black public elementary school did not possess a sufficient number of computers to serve its enrollment adequately. Through funding sources, a state-of-the-art computer education center was created at the youth club with the condition that the youth club staff involve low-income parents of the youngsters in the program.

Initially, the center staff discerned little visible parent support for the computer education program. In talking with parents the staff made two important discoveries. First, parents did not fully understand or appreciate the educational thrust that the computer education program represented. That is, parents did not realize that the youth club possessed better computer equipment and intended to provide better computer instruction than was available in the neighborhood elementary school. Second, the staff discovered that a group of influential parents viewed the club's computer program as duplicating the school program, which they found deficient in terms of access and instruction. A number of other parents confided that their interaction with school personnel regarding their children's performance was seldom positive. Several parents disclosed that they had negative experiences in school when they were growing up. The challenge confronting the center's computer education staff was thus to break this cycle of negative transactions that were associated with both school and apparently any kind of formal instruction.

Reviews of the parental involvement literature (Becher, 1984; Henderson, 1987) suggest that parental involvement activity usually consists of a home-school dyad. Generally, a model of parental involvement emerges in which the parent's intrinsic interest in the child is the basis for some kind of intervention. In other words, the target is the parent, and by influencing the parent the child's achievement or school success is generally positively affected. That is, the route to greater child participation is achieved by gaining parental participation.

It was obvious to the computer education staff that the route to greater child participation through parents was not feasible due to their previous negative experiences with schools. The staff attended a parental involvement workshop based on Cochran's (1987) empowerment principles and decided to try to operationalize "valuing the parent" as a means to encourage parental participation. They hit upon the idea that genuine valuing of the child was perhaps the surest way to communicate valuing of the parent. The staff decided to develop an instructional approach within the center that would promote learning success. The success would then be coupled with recognition of youngsters' efforts and accomplishments, and parents would then be invited to share in their children's achievements. Thus, in this approach the route to the parents was through their children.

While this indirect method of parental instruction, achieved by first teaching computer skills to youngsters, is not commonplace in educational circles, Nickse (1990) has identified this approach as one of the four basic adult-learning models by which educational services can be delivered. She characterizes this type of intervention as a "direct child-indirect adult" approach. While the child is the main recipient of direct instruction (oftentimes through special programs like Chapter 1 of the Elementary and Secondary Education Act, P.L. 100-297), parents are not recipients, at least initially. Parental interest, support, and participation heavily depend on their skills and self-confidence. Similar to Lightfoot's (1978) adaptive strategy approach, Nickse advocates making sure parents feel accepted and are given special consideration, which may include modifying programs and approaches. Tailoring programs to the specific adult clientele seems the best way to ensure that parents become colearners in the educational endeavors of their children.

The staff's overarching goals were first to ensure that youngsters engaged in successful learning, and second to acknowledge their success appropriately. A number of strategies were devised to promote these goals. Individual progress was noted regularly, and significant accomplishments received special recognition. Work was displayed on bulletin boards both within the center and on the encased bulletin board at the building's entrance, certificates of achievement were awarded, and children's names and achievements were mentioned in a weekly newsletter.

The striking difference between after-school and during-school programs is that the former are voluntary. The youth agency serves children ranging from six to eighteen years of age, and hours for participation have age restrictions. That is, any child may drop in on his or her own volition according to regularly posted times and participate in the day's activities. (The computer center was open from 3:30 to 8:15 P.M.) Thus, the experience has to be perceived as positive, and the child has to be and feel successful in order to want to return to the center. The environment and the attitudes and behavior of the staff were therefore crucial. The center's environment was attractive, orderly, and conducive to learning. Learners, upon entering the center, had rights and responsibilities. Children might help each other, but they could not interfere with each other's learning. They had control over computers and materials, and the atmosphere was friendly. The staff was helpful and intentionally nonevaluative and noncritical.

Most of the time children competed against themselves. For example, their progress in keyboarding or typing was recorded on a regular basis, and they received staff praise when they could type the entire alphabet via the touch system, or when they typed ten words a minute. Because working at the computer for the most part was self-instructional, youngsters of different ages could be learning the same material (for example, learning to type) without embarrassment. When the fifteen-words-per-minute level was reached, the child was awarded a certificate of achievement. When the thirty-word criterion was reached, the child's picture was taken, labeled, and displayed in the showcase located at the building's entrance for all to see.

Youngsters who mastered skills and progressed successfully and rapidly through programs were encouraged to help those who were beginners or having difficulty. Ten youngsters were invited to serve as center computer aides and were paid stipends or minimum hourly wage for assisting the center's staff or for serving as computer skills tutors to less able youngsters after school and during summer school programs. These tutors were recognized through feature articles published in the computer center's newsletter.

The combination of the youngsters acquiring the various computer competencies and the procedure for recognizing their achievement kindled further interest, effort, and accomplishment. The process gave the youngsters a sense of empowerment. They knew they had acquired knowledge, skills, and abilities that were visible when they completed programs and assignments or helped peers. Mostly, they were eager to share their knowledge and skills and were encouraged to discuss their progress at home.

Involving Parents in the Educational Process

Once the payoff/recognition approach for youngsters was underway, ways to kindle parent awareness, interest, and involvement were undertaken. Parents were informed of their youngsters' progress by receiving desktop-published newsletters with children's names and pictures. When a significant achievement milestone was reached, letters were sent to the parents inviting them to the center to attend recognition and award ceremonies honoring their children. When they visited the center, parents were given a guided tour, invited to observe youngsters busily engaged in computer lessons, and encouraged to learn how to operate a computer or how to type and to review popular computer software programs. Parents were given the option of participating alone or with their child.

Parents were told that their comments and views were always welcome. Children regularly displayed their new computer skills to their parents, and parents were encouraged to engage in hands-on participation. A key strategy in nurturing parental participation was keeping procedures for participation simple and informal. A parent drop-in program was developed. That is, any parent could drop in at the center unannounced, and a staff member would assist the parent in getting started or in continuing a previous lesson. The parent had the option of reserving a computer at a specific time but did not have to inform the staff if the reservation could not be honored. Parents who made a reservation were given an appointment card. Parents were told that they could come by themselves or they could invite a friend to participate. Written flyers announcing computer-training workshops were distributed in the neighborhood, including the elementary school's office, and a special invitation to parents was included. Over time parents began to see how computers might benefit their lives. All parental requests or special needs were honored if at all possible. Parental requests that were honored included typing and word-processing lessons and access and assistance for typing personal letters, devising and creating large banners for special occasions, printing of original greeting cards, designing, printing, and constructing buttons, composing and printing newsletters, creating print-outs of telephone lists, and printing certificates.

During the first year of operation of the computer center approximately 110 upper-elementary and middle-school youngsters participated in the computer activities and spent time after school in the center on a regular basis. Parental interest was sporadic, and parents sometimes did not attend award ceremonies for the children. The center staff, nevertheless, sent certificates home describing the child's achievement and a note encouraging the parent to attend the next ceremony. During the first six months of operation, a total of eleven parents visited the center. Five of these individuals returned regularly to learn computer skills. Each time they were reminded that they could bring a friend on their next visit. By the end of the year approximately twenty-five parents frequented the center to receive instruction or to accomplish personal tasks or projects. One of the parents became so interested and skillful, she volunteered to serve as a computer center assistant.

Lessons Learned from the Involvement of Parents

Involving low-income, minority parents as observers or as colearners in the educational process of their children is a constant challenge. The ever-present cultural diversity between undereducated parents and well-educated, computer-proficient center staff seemed always a potential distancing rather than unifying factor if not kept in mind. It is far too easy *not* to see and understand the perspectives of parents concerning not only their own personal educational experience but also that of their children. Schools probably are remiss in realizing the critical impact that previous educational experiences of parents play in their own continuing education and in the education of their children. It appears that the staff's preconception about the valuable role and contribution that a child's parent can and must play in the educational process kept the staff on track. Including parents and winning their support by responding flexibly and creatively to them as adults who possessed a need for continuing education were certainly key factors in the success of the center.

By focusing initially on children's successful learning, this project provides support for the direct child-indirect adult model advocated by Nickse (1990) for involving low-income parents in the educational process. The model underscores the mutually reinforcing effect that parents and children can have on each other's educational outcomes. The parents share in the child's achievements, which are sources of parental pride and satisfaction. While children were acquiring computer skills, the positive, informal atmosphere and unrestricted drop-in policy seemed to promote active parental participation. Ensuring that the parents feel welcome and soliciting their comments and reactions go far in breaking down any possible communication barriers. Once parents see the application of computer skills and technology through children's performance and achievement, flexible schedules to accommodate parental participation make learning opportunities attractive. Enabling parents to produce concrete outcomes such as telephone rosters results in their staunch support of the educational program. And learning and education become a high priority in the home. When this occurs, the instructor, the parent, and the child become colearners in the educational process. Valuing parents both as parents and as adult learners and believing that their involvement is an asset instead of a liability provide the foundation for meaningful, interactive involvement by low-income parents.

Involvement of low-income parents in the educational process requires reversal of a long history of alienation from the school and of deliberate noninvolvement. The experience of this project and the findings of Comer (1988) bear this out. Significant parental involvement in the computer education program was achieved only after a full year of diligent effort. The development of positive interaction between parents and educators requires that the latter not only view the world from the perspective of parents but also provide encouragement and support to enhance the role and involvement of parents in the educational process.

References

Becher, R. M. *Parent Involvement: A Review of Research and Principles of Successful Practice.* Report no. 400-83-0021. Washington, D.C.: National Institute of Education, 1984.

Bialo, E. R., and Sivin, J. P. "Computers and At-Risk Youth: A Partial Solution to a Complex Problem." *Classroom Computer Learning,* 1989, *5,* 36–39.

Bronfenbrenner, U. *A Report on Longitudinal Evaluations of Preschool Programs.* Vol. 2: *Is Early Intervention Effective?* Publication no. (OHD) 74-25. Washington, D.C.: Office of Child Development, Department of Health, Education, and Welfare, 1974.

Cavazos, L. F. *Educating Our Children: Parents and Schools Together. A Report to the President.* Washington, D.C.: Government Printing Office, 1965. (ED 015 328)

Cochran, M. "The Parental Empowerment Process: Building on Family Strengths." *Equity and Choice,* 1987, *4* (1), 9–23.

Cochran, M., and Henderson, C. R., Jr., *Family Matters: Evaluation of the Parental Empowerment Program.* Summary of a final report to the National Institute of Education. Ithaca, N.Y.: Department of Home Economics, Cornell University, 1986.

Cohen, D. K. "Policy for Public Schools: Compensation and Integration." *Harvard Education Review,* 1968, *38* (1), 114–137.

Coleman, J. *Equality of Educational Opportunity.* Washington, D.C.: Government Printing Office, 1966.

Comer, J. P. "Educating Poor Minority Children." *Scientific American,* 1988, *259* (5), 42–48.

Comer, J. P. "Parent Participation in Schools: The School Development Program Model." *Family Resource Coalition Report,* 1989, *8* (2), 4–6.

Fantini, M. D. "Discussion." *Harvard Education Review,* 1968, *38* (1), 160–175.

Henderson, A. T. (ed.). *The Evidence Continues to Grow (Parent Involvement Improves Student Achievement).* Columbia, Md.: National Committee for Citizens in Education, 1987.

Henderson, A. T. "Parents Are a School's Best Friends." *Phi Delta Kappan,* 1988, *70* (2), 148–153.

Hughes, J. "A Commitment to Parent Education." In *Families and Schools: Implement-*

ing Parent Education. Report no. 121. Denver, Colo.: Education Commission of the States, 1979.

Lightfoot, S. L. *Worlds Apart: Relationship Between Families and School.* New York: Basic Books, 1978.

McLaughlin, M. W., and Shields, P. M. "Involving Low-Income Parents in the Schools: A Role for Policy?" *Phi Delta Kappan,* 1987, *69* (2), 156–160.

Mayor's Advisory Panel on Decentralization. *Reconnection for Learning: A Community School System for New York City.* New York: Mayor's Advisory Panel on Decentralization, 1967.

Moles, O. C. "Who Wants Parent Involvement?" *Education and Urban Society,* 1987, *19* (2), 137–145.

Nickse, R. S. "Family Literacy Programs: Ideas for Action." *Adult Learning,* 1990, *41* (2), 9–29.

Schlossman, S. "Before Home-Start: Notes Toward a History of Parent Education in America, 1897–1929." *Harvard Education Review,* 1976, *46* (3), 436–467.

Tyack, D. B. *The One Best System: A History of American Urban Education.* Cambridge, Mass.: Harvard University Press, 1974.

Wilensky, R., and Kline, D. M. *Renewing Urban School: The Community Connection.* Denver, Colo.: Education Commission of the States, 1988.

Frank E. Nardine is associate professor of educational psychology at the University of Wisconsin, Milwaukee, and chair of Families as Educators, a special interest group of the American Educational Research Association.

The process linked to the community education concept provides a framework whereby the learning needs of a culturally diverse society can be correctly identified and addressed.

Community Education: A Culturally Responsive Approach to Learning

Diane Buck Briscoe

Imagine a society in which individual learning is a natural and ongoing process. Imagine a society in which agencies freely work together and school buildings are open more often than they are closed. Envision bustling communities within neighborhoods of involved individuals: working, learning, and relaxing together. In such communities, the ideals of community education would have been realized. Community education in its purest form would be in evidence.

Community education is a concept that defines an appropriate process for addressing the needs of a culturally diverse society. The process seeks to integrate community and learning in such a way that they are extensions of each other and equal partners. Community education espouses a way of life that involves people working together in total partnership to identify an ideal and a means of realizing it.

This chapter provides a brief historical perspective on the development of community education, explores the elements contained in the process, and describes two dominant models of community education and two exemplary programs that have successfully incorporated the elements of community education in activities serving culturally diverse populations.

A Historical Perspective

Community education is not a novel concept, even though the focus on it in recent years would lead one to believe otherwise. Examples of community education can be seen in the activities of the late nineteenth- and early twentieth-centuries, such as settlement houses, the movement toward pioneering and westward settlement, and the Depression era New Deal programs. The enclaves of prehistoric peoples, the African-American slave communities in the United States, and the early Native American communities also exhibited many of the principles that are considered integral to the concept of community education today (Sinclair, 1983; Richardson and Decker, 1985; Minzey, 1974; DeLargy, 1989).

The common element found throughout these periods was the opportunity for individuals to gain knowledge and skills through active participation in the essential tasks of communal life. Learning often resembled modern-day work-experience programs. Relevant experiences ensured the economic survival of the individual and thus contributed to the common good and well-being of the community. This approach to learning began early in life. It provided participants with a vehicle through which they were able to engage in the work of the family and the community. The process enabled participants to understand the culture and value system of their communities and provided the communities with an opportunity to reward participation (Sinclair, 1983).

The urbanization of the nation in the 1940s rapidly rendered this form of community education obsolete. The time spent in a single community interacting and learning was eroded through improved mobility. The messages and values imparted through the electronic media often conflicted with traditional family and community customs. The centralization of basic services and the large numbers of mothers working outside the home were other factors that contributed to a shift away from communities as the locus of social control (Sinclair, 1983). Additionally, an increasingly complex technology led to education being acquired through professionally trained individuals rather than through traditional methods.

The undermining of community cohesion has been exacerbated by other societal changes as well. For example, in terms of fundamental features of economic and social life, many communities have moved from being agrarian to industrial, rural to urban, mainstream to minority, "melting pot" to "salad bowl," youth-oriented to senior-focused, and personal to impersonal. The standards and values that once served as unifying and solidifying elements in communities have often been overshadowed by individualism and lack of collective responsibility. The family no longer singularly reflects the intact nuclear unit of earlier periods. Family groups are often spread across states rather than centered in a single geographical community.

The changes that have occurred in certain minority communities have been particularly acute. Increases in crime rates, teenager birth rates, substance abuse, and the purported disintegration of the "family" have been the subjects of almost daily media coverage. African-Americans, Hispanics, and Native Americans are disengaging from almost all levels of formal education at a steady pace. Unemployment rates remain disproportionately high in urban areas and in many minority communities, especially among the male, teenaged segments of these populations. Chapter One offers details on many of the statistics regarding these phenomena. However, one often overlooked perspective is that many of these changes may be the secondary effects of institutional practices, governmental policies, and administrative decision-making processes that did not comprehensively include a cross-section of representatives from the affected communities (Nance, 1989).

For example, urban renewal has often dismantled viable neighborhoods and minority-owned businesses under the guise of progress. The red-lining policies of lending institutions have often made it difficult for individuals in these targeted areas to acquire loans. Frequently, the red-lined areas are disproportionately populated by minorities. The relocation of mainstream businesses from inner-city areas to remote sections of many communities and the lack of affordable and convenient mass transportation have often limited the access of many minorities to employment. The closing of African-American high schools in minority communities and the reassignment of their minority principals to vice-principalships in other communities have eliminated both central gathering points and highly visible role models for many minorities. Institutional practices in education applied to African-American, Hispanic, and Native American youth, such as tracking, may be short-circuiting the development of many present and future community leaders (Fraga, Meier, and England, 1986; Darling-Hammond, 1985; Colburn and Adcock, 1989). These are but a few examples of the practices whose consequences have been disastrous for many minority communities.

The strength of any community is determined by the degree to which its members share standards, values, and interests. Accommodation and comradery are unifying elements that offer to community members the sense of solidarity necessary for cohesion. Many of these unifying elements have been eroded in the communities of today (Clark, 1987; Fletcher, 1987; Kerensky, 1982).

A grasp of the term "community" is vital to any understanding of the concept of community education (Minzey, 1974), but an adequate definition of the term has proved elusive (Clark, 1987; Fletcher, 1987). Further, the nature of most communities is fluid, with constant movement and change. Because the idea of community is not finite, the assumptions made relative to it are thus also fluid.

Notions of what community means are derived from the knowledge bases, experiences, and moral, ideological, and philosophical perspectives of the observers (Clark, 1987; Fletcher, 1987). Over the years, the boundaries of definition have become increasingly blurred, causing both theoretical and professional confusion. For example, today the boundaries of a community can be defined geographically, socially, religiously, culturally, or professionally. These factors add a subjective element to attempts to define the term, hindering the acceptance of a universal definition of it. Within the context of this chapter the term "community" is used to refer both to an area of geography, defined by specified boundaries, and to a unit of people, cohesively bound through commonly shared values, standards, and goals.

Community Education

Definitions tend to serve as a guide by which practice is measured. The inability to singularly define the term community may have contributed to an inability to establish a definition of and universal philosophical base for the concept of community education. The resulting functional ambiguity has favored inclusion rather than exclusion in regard to the category of community education programs. For our purposes here, community education is seen as a concept that encourages lifelong learning through a process requiring maximum utilization of existing resources, participatory decision making, and collaboration with agencies and individuals sharing similar goals.

Community education requires responsiveness. Its process demands action, constant analysis, critique, and review. These requirements have sometimes precluded the easy operationalization of the concept (Allen, Bastiani, Martin, and Richards, 1987). Furthermore, communities' perceptions of needs and the perceptions of those in formal positions of leadership have sometimes been in direct conflict.

The inability to find a universally acceptable definition of community education, the inconsistent operationalization of the term, and the inclusion of programs that do not correctly represent the community education model have influenced the development of the concept and influenced the process, often subtly. However, the community education process still provides a viable approach whereby the analysis and diagnosis of needs and the prescription of solutions are widely applicable. Community education also offers a framework whereby culturally diverse communities can respond positively to change, and many issues faced by society can be addressed (Kowalski and Fallon, 1986; Bryant, 1989). The community education model is one of empowerment when properly implemented, for the process fosters self-actualization and self-sufficiency. Pallas, Natriello, and McDill (1989) suggest that while learning certainly takes place within the framework of formal schooling, the family and community also play a vital role.

Research utilizing quantitative or qualitative methodology to determine the effectiveness of the community education process is sparse (Allen, Bastiani, Martin, and Richards, 1987; Wilcox, 1989; Roudebush, 1987). This paucity of research and data may be owing to the manner in which community education has developed. Much of that development has generally been policy or practice led (Allen, Bastiani, Martin, and Richards, 1987). Research related to the effectiveness of the process with culturally diverse populations is especially sparse. Available data seem to indicate that opportunities for formal learning are often provided to those economically and educationally advantaged populations who are best equipped to obtain it for themselves (Heisel, 1986; Wilcox, 1989). However, African-American and disadvantaged learners with little formal education have been shown to respond favorably to programs that meet their needs. This is especially true when the programs are offered in nonformal settings and encompass nontraditional learning (Heisel, 1986; Briscoe and Ross, 1989).

Attempts to achieve consensus on a universal vision for community education have been more successful. Few would disagree with the goal of providing relevant learning opportunities, lifelong, through a process of citizen involvement. In this regard, two models of community education seem to dominate. These are the community-based comprehensive model and the school-based model. The two models have many attributes in common, but they also manifest several differences (Roudebush, 1987).

Comprehensive Model. Certain commonly held principles of the most frequently utilized, community-based comprehensive model of community education have remained constant, which may have contributed to the ongoing viability of the concept (Allen, Bastiani, Martin, and Richards, 1987). These principles are briefly explained below:

The *participatory decision-making processes* of community education ensure that those who are most affected by an issue are instrumental in identifying needs and in planning, developing, and implementing appropriate solutions. This approach ensures responsiveness. It also fosters leadership development and aids empowerment by allowing participants to learn and develop requisite skills for self-determination.

Learning is a continuous process that begins at birth and ends at death. This process of *lifelong learning* can occur in formal and nonformal settings and allows individuals to become self-actualized. The opportunity to learn is viewed as a right that should be made available to all, regardless of race, ethnicity, or social status.

Maximization of existing fiscal, human, and physical resources is a means of achieving cost-effectiveness. This approach enhances the feasibility of providing activities in almost all localities and often eliminates long delays for appropriations, construction, or staffing. Ownership and increased visibility for programs are also enhanced.

Ease of access to activities increases participation and responsiveness by those being targeted. The availability of activities in close proximity to participants fosters community interaction, encourages ownership of the programs by the neighborhood, and strengthens the bonds of the community.

Collaboration and cooperation with agencies that have similar goals and that share similar clientele ensure an integrated delivery system (Beder, 1984). This collaboration capitalizes on the strengths of existing agencies and organizations and discourages duplication of effort. This approach also maximizes the efficiency of each entity and promotes cost-effectiveness.

School-Based Model. While similar in many respects to the community-based comprehensive model of community education, the school-based model utilizes the school as the focal point for administering and coordinating program activities. This model of community education advocates a close partnership between community and school.

Community education, in the context of the school setting, lends elements of flexibility, acceptability, and innovation to what many perceive as a formidable and rigid bureaucracy: the school (Allen, Bastiani, Martin, and Richards, 1987; Gehret, 1987). Proponents of the school-based model emphasize that school buildings are in close proximity to almost every neighborhood, are owned by citizens because of their tax support, and provide a central vehicle by which the community education process can be facilitated.

The framework for the most visible and commonly practiced school-based model was conceived in Flint, Michigan. The activities associated with this model resulted from the philanthropy of Charles Stewart Mott and his collaborative efforts with Frank Manley (Campbell, 1972). The activities that contributed to making this school-based model exemplary and worthy of attention included the use of a paid community education coordinator, the creation of community councils and block clubs, the integral involvement of the community in the school, the organizational plan for administering programs, and the dissemination procedures utilized (Campbell, 1972). The basic beliefs and principles that guide community education in the school setting are as follows:

1. Learning is a lifelong process and an integral part of living.
2. Community involvement is a community right that leads to better decisions and thus to increased community support.
3. The best approach to improving the larger community is to improve the smaller community.
4. Every community has an abundance of untapped educational resources that can be utilized to improve educational effectiveness.
5. Education and schooling should be all-inclusive and extend beyond what is provided during the prescribed school day (Minzey, 1974).

Community Education Programs

Two programs in particular are considered here since they reflect exemplary practice in community education. They have been in existence for a number of years and specifically serve large numbers of underserved, culturally diverse individuals. Both programs have been replicated as successful models. The first program represents the comprehensive, community-based approach to community education. The second represents the school-based model of community education espoused by Charles Stewart Mott.

Both programs are located in a sprawling urban area, but the concepts and principles contributing to their success could be applied in any community. The comradery and esprit de corps often found in small, rural communities would perhaps make the programs even easier to implement in those environments.

Youth Action Program (YAP). The success of the Youth Action Program in the Harlem community of New York City (Youth Action Program, 1985) is especially heartening in that the original participants and the majority of those involved today are young, primarily Hispanic and African-American males. This population tends to be viewed negatively by society and to experience the highest rates of unemployment and disengagement from formal education.

YAP was conceived in 1978 after a meeting between a young Hispanic male and a social worker. This young man, not yet sixteen years of age, was unemployed, disengaged from school, and living independently of his family with twelve of his friends in an abandoned building. By conventional standards, the group was homeless. From that initial meeting and a later agreement evolved a multimillion dollar program, governed primarily by young Hispanic and African-American male adults who were community residents (Belkin, 1983). Participants in YAP gut and renovate abandoned buildings. When completed, the top floors of the buildings are used as affordable housing for community residents and the lower floors are rented to the public.

The collaborative aspect of the program is amply illustrated by the agencies that became involved in the program's implementation. The city contributed a building. YAP, the Federal Law Enforcement Assistance Administration, city banks, and religious institutions also provided various resources. Resources were also forthcoming through the Comprehensive Employment and Training Act. Previously, no city tax levy funds had been earmarked for youth employment; however, over a five-year period, the amount contributed to the Youth Action Program totaled almost $60 million.

The participatory decision-making processes of community education are illustrated in numerous ways by YAP. The premise from the beginning of the program was that the idleness of young people results from economic and societal barriers. Consequently, the vision of YAP has been to instill confidence by providing the skills needed to address problems, and to affirm and validate the ideas and abilities of the participants. Particular efforts have been undertaken to avoid turning the participants into "clients." Policy decisions have been made by the participants in the program, with counsel from adult organizers.

Ease of access is an essential component of the program. Participants live, learn, and work in the community. The local base is essential in that concern about the community provides impetus for the involvement of the participants in positive change. Their creative energies are channeled into the home community, are visible to the community, and are reinforced by the community.

Opportunities for lifelong learning have been presented in a variety of ways. Initially, local professionals taught participants the necessary technical and construction skills (Belkin, 1983). Participants received no salary but were given an opportunity to prove something to others. A general equivalency diploma component was added since many of the participants had disengaged from school. Counseling and leadership development activities were included. Empowerment through decision making and the visible results of goals attained have instilled in participants a sense of achievement and self-respect.

Middle College High School (MCHS). The continually increasing dropout rates in secondary education, particularly among Native Americans, African-Americans, and certain Hispanic populations, have necessitated innovative strategies by local school districts. Many school districts have offered alternative programs under the sponsorship of adult education to more efficiently address the needs of students at risk of disengaging from school. Frequently, formal adult education programs have been utilized for young adults who have disengaged from secondary education but who wish to acquire literacy skills or the high school diploma. Middle College High School, in Long Island, New York, offers an example of a model that could be replicated by these districts. This program also adheres to many of the principles appropriate to the school-based model of community education.

In its fifteen-year existence, MCHS has identified high-risk students and given them responsibility for decisions affecting their lives. The school has an enrollment of five hundred students in grades ten through twelve and represents a collaborative effort between the New York City Board of Education, the New York City Board of Higher Education, and LaGuardia Community College. The results of this program have been a dropout rate of 15 percent and a graduation rate of 85 percent. Over 75 percent of graduating seniors continue on to college.

Fifty percent of the population for whom these successes are occurring is composed of educationally underserved minorities: Hispanic and African-American. The students can be considered nontraditional learners in that many are older than the traditional student would be for the same grade. The program attempts to prevent disengagement from school by accepting referrals from counselors in feeder schools. The criteria used for referral include frequent absences from school, a record of family problems, and evidence of psychological or physical abuse.

These young adults are involved in decision making in many ways. Criteria for admission into the school are determined by a team that is largely composed of currently enrolled students. Peer counselors serve as a judicial forum to hear student grievances. Students are treated as responsible young adults, capable of making decisions and accepting the consequences of those decisions. In most instances, processes of adult learning have been utilized. Consequently, peer pressure is often exerted when abuses of perceived freedoms are evidenced.

Positive attitudes toward lifelong learning are shaped through the structure of the educational program. The curriculum conforms to the requirements of the New York City Board of Education and the New York State Board of Education; however, the principal of the school carries a department chair designation at LaGuardia Community College.

Within the curriculum requirements are a wide range of choices that give students a feeling of control over their educational plans. Student progress is self-paced and the curriculum is based on individual student needs and abilities. Smaller class sizes are economically feasible because the number of students who are absent from classes is considerably lower in this program. Self-directed learning is fostered in this atmosphere.

Adult educators believe that learning is a preparation for living. The school-based community education model views education as encompassing more than the prescribed instruction offered in most school curricula. The program at MCHS incorporates these two perspectives through the provision of eleven group guidance sessions covering topics such as drugs, sex, and family problems. The sessions are offered daily. No academic credit is given for guidance sessions, and no subject is considered too delicate to discuss.

A community involvement component incorporates career preparation and provides students an opportunity to bond with and to develop a sense of responsibility for their communities and the members in them. Through three nonpaid internships, young people are allowed to experience the "real world." Preparation for the internship includes an in-school preparatory course. On-site supervision is included. Internships must be completed prior to graduation; consequently, students graduate with a diploma and with a resumé as well.

The high school and community college collaboration is an important model for encouraging high-risk young adults to complete their education. High school students are allowed to take college-level courses, but credit is deferred until high school completion.

Conclusion

The process of community education effectively addresses the needs of a culturally diverse society. The learning strategies deemed effective for adult learners (Knowles, 1970; Seaman and Fellenz, 1989; Cross, 1981) are compatible with those advocated for adults in community education settings. The community education process does not require that differences be suppressed, yet successes are achieved. The result is empowerment for those who participate in the process. Community education provides a framework whereby all participants have an opportunity for self-actualization. Community education offers a vehicle through which the communities of today can find strength in their diversity.

References

Allen, G., Bastiani, J., Martin, I., and Richards, K. (eds.). *Community Education—An Agenda for Education Reform*. Milton Keynes, England: Open University Educational Enterprises, 1987.

Beder, H. (ed.). *Realizing the Potential of Interorganizational Cooperation*. New Directions for Continuing Education, no. 23. San Francisco: Jossey-Bass, 1984.

Belkin, L. "Youths Restore Building and Rebuild Own Pride." *New York Times*, Sept. 26, 1983, sec. B3.

Briscoe, D. B., and Ross, J. M. "Racial and Ethnic Minorities and Adult Education." In S. B. Merriam and P. M. Cunningham (eds.), *Handbook of Adult and Continuing Education*. San Francisco: Jossey-Bass, 1989.

Bryant, L. "Today's Communities: Getting to Know You." *Community Education Journal*, 1989, *16* (4), 4-5.

Campbell, C. M. "Contributions of the Mott Foundation to the Community Education Movement." *Phi Delta Kappan*, 1972, *54* (3), 195-197.

Clark, D. "The Concept of Community Education." In G. Allen, J. Bastiani, I. Martin, and K. Richards (eds.), *Community Education—An Agenda for Education Reform*. Milton Keynes, England: Open University Educational Enterprises, 1987.

Colburn, J., and Adcock, B. "Community Education and the Native American Community." *Community Education Journal*, 1989, *16* (4), 14-16.

Cross, K. P. (ed.). *Adults as Learners: Increasing Participation and Facilitating Learning*. San Francisco: Jossey-Bass, 1981.

Darling-Hammond, L. *Equality and Excellence: The Educational Status of Black Americans*. New York: College Board Publications, 1985.

DeLargy, P. F. "Public Schools and Community Education." In S. B. Merriam and P. M. Cunningham (eds.), *Handbook of Adult and Continuing Education*. San Francisco: Jossey-Bass, 1989.

Fletcher, C. "The Meanings of 'Community' in Community Education." In G. Allen, J. Bastiani, I. Martin, and K. Richards (eds.), *Community Education—An Agenda for Education Reform*. Milton Keynes, England: Open University Educational Enterprises, 1987.

Fraga, L., Meier, K., and England, R. "Hispanic Americans and Educational Policy: Limits to Equal Access." *Journal of Politics*, 1986, *48*, 851-876.

Gehret, E. F. "Do Community Schools Improve Citizen Attitudes Toward School?" *Community Education Research Digest*, 1987, *2* (1), 9-23.

Heisel, M. A. "Learning Activities of Disadvantaged Older Adults." *Community Education Research Digest*, 1986, *1* (1), 14-21.

Kerensky, V. M. "Community Educators: The High Touch People." In *Community Education Bulletin*. Occasional paper (June). Boca Raton: Florida Atlantic University, 1982.

Knowles, M. S. *The Modern Practice of Adult Education: Andragogy Versus Pedagogy*. New York: Association Press, 1970.

Kowalski, T. J., and Fallon, J. A. *Community Education: Processes and Programs*. Fastback 243. Bloomington, Ind.: Phi Delta Kappan Educational Foundation, 1986.

Minzey, J. D. "Community Education—Another Perception." *Community Education Journal*, 1974, *4* (3), 7, 58-61.

Nance, E. E. "The Black Community and the Leadership Dilemma." *Community Education Journal*, 1989, *16* (4), 10-11.

Pallas, A. M., Natriello, G., and McDill, E. L. "The Changing Nature of the Disadvantaged Population, Current Dimensions and Future Trends." *Educational Researcher*, 1989, *18* (5), 16-22.

Richardson, M. B., and Decker, L. E. *The Learning Community*. Alexandria, Va.: National Community Education Association, 1985.

Roudebush, D. "Community Education: A Comparison of Theory and Practice." *Community Education Research Digest*, 1987, 2 (1), 24-37.

Seaman, D., and Fellenz, R. *Effective Strategies for Teaching Adults*. Columbus, Ohio: Merrill, 1989.

Sinclair, R. L. (ed.). *For Every School a Community: Expanding Environments for Learning*. Boston: Institute for Responsive Learning, 1983.

Wilcox, D. D. "Perceived Participation in Community Education of Secondary Students and Minority Students in Colorado." *Community Education Research Digest*, 1989, *4* (1), 41-46.

Youth Action Program. "Youth Action in East Harlem." *Youth Policy*, 1985, 7 (9).

Diane Buck Briscoe is assistant professor of adult education at the University of South Florida, Tampa. She formerly served as the director of the university's Center for Community Education.

Some programs of adult education in the minority community that use the concept of popular education are reviewed. The different dimensions of popular education are explained, as well as how these dimensions affect the educational system by giving the participants a greater and more active role in it.

Popular Education: Models That Contribute to the Empowerment of Learners in Minority Communities

Jorge Jeria

The historical roots of popular education extend back as far as the French Revolution. As Mejia (1989, p. 148) has observed, "the term Popular Education has come to us as participants of a Western culture transformed in a political act by the French Revolution and it has extended until today as a conflict in the educational process between those who defend and prolong the official and those who fight the construction of a new hegemony, social and political." Since education was a privilege in prerevolutionary France, the idea of extending educational opportunities to all citizens was an important outcome of the revolution (Pollard, 1957). It is interesting to note that this advanced thought in France regarding universal primary school was declared obligatory only in 1832. But still, as a result of the French Revolution and its educational reforms, the concept of democratization in education or "education for all" was introduced.

The emergence of the United States in North America, founded on many of the ideals of the French Revolution, brought only isolated efforts to develop the type of popular education proposed in France, England, and Switzerland in the late eighteenth century. Overall, in the United States, the development of an educational system was decidedly racist in character since it was divided from its early stages onward between Blacks and Whites, especially in the South. As a direct result of discriminatory practices, "Negro" schools were created in the South following the Civil War. Education for Blacks, however, has been but one forum in the constant struggle for equality in the economic, social, and political spheres of American life.

The education of Black adults and children was in its very essence popular education. It was not an education proposed by the state but rather a type of education that confronted the status quo in order to achieve integration. A good case-in-point of the tradition of popular education was the development in 1932 in Tennessee of the Highlander Folk School. Highlander brought together many leaders of the civil rights movement in an organized effort to challenge the official system of education proposed by the state (Adams and Horton, 1975). In other words, given the poor living and working conditions in the urban industrial areas of the northeastern United States and in the agricultural fields of the South, organizations set up by Blacks to fight illiteracy, poverty, and inequality carried a strong political message to the educational systems in place. Indeed, the alternative systems of popular education are still prevalent since state-endorsed educational practices continue to foster inequality.

There are many examples of popular education today in the United States. The literacy project of the Bay Area in California is an example of a movement for ethnic and minority education and organization. Another example is the Tenant Management Program in Chicago, conducted under the auspices of the Lindeman Center of Northern Illinois University. Also, the master's degree program for community leaders in the Hispanic community of Chicago, offered by the faculty of adult education at Northern Illinois University, illustrates popular education. The concept of popular education in these cases can be analyzed in terms of their methodological components, thus clarifying the practice of popular education. Popular education includes sociocultural, political, democratic, and humanistic dimensions. It is necessary to understand these dimensions in order to understand the concept of popular education and to appreciate its contribution to the empowerment of learners in minority communities.

The Concept of Popular Education

Sociocultural Dimension. We can observe that while educational systems may carry the signs of democratization, if they are managed by culturally dominant agents, the ability to suppress "culturally excluded" populations still remains. We can point to three elements in society that indicate that the sociopolitical structure does not respond to the excluded groups: (1) the development of an authoritarian culture, (2) the incapacity of the political party system to respond to the demands of the population, and (3) a state unable to respond to the needs of the so-called new actors (members of minority groups). An authoritarian culture is reflected and manifested, for instance, in the relationships among students in a school, the relationships between students and teachers, and the relationships at work between employees and bosses. These relationships tend to reinforce all the aspects of domination in society that exclude and restrict freedom.

Political and Democratic Dimension. Popular education has a profound political and democratic dimension. For example, under the Reagan administration, the government abandoned many social programs, thereby leaving space for many popular organizations to take the role that was earlier the responsibility of the state. In this case we can say that popular education is more than just political action (as proposed by the state) as it becomes an alternative form of development.

Popular education takes a political form inasmuch as it is conceived from the unique experiences and realities of the participants rather than from curricula established by the state. An important element in many of the popular education programs is the rejection of authoritarianism in the educational system, as well as in the economic and political systems (Vio Grossi, 1989). It is also important to understand that popular education questions the neutrality of conventional education and, consequently, provides the political option of democratizing political power and making profound inroads in the social distribution of knowledge. Thus, popular education rejects the vertical structure of education between the learner and the instructor by proposing a dialogue as an alternative. This, in turn, undermines traditional vertical or hierarchical policies that do not promote equal access to and participation in education. Therefore, democratization takes place.

Humanistic Dimension. Education from the vertical perspective is basically uniform because it does not allow for diversity. But even with diverse experiences, education in the United States is typically presented in a universal fashion, which does not allow for this diversity to be integrated into the curricula. From this point in view, we can say that popular education makes possible the participation of all those who are excluded from the benefits of education because of inadequate education. In this sense, minority and indigenous groups have clearly stated the issue of self-determination. Their collective struggle covers a whole array of issues, such as tribal rights to natural resources, preservation of languages and cultures, and resistance to the attempts of mainstream society to integrate them into the lower strata of the modern economy (Prajuli, 1988).

Popular Education and Its Practice

Local Versus State Model. When an option is possible between the professional educator and the local community, a new modality develops known as "alternative education." The principle that guides this option is the implementation of a participative process in the design, practice, and evaluation of an educational project from the beneficiaries' point of view. It is characterized by "Freirean positions": (1) the desire to be engaged in political participation and (2) the desire to be a part of the decision-making process from an autonomous point of view (Ormeno, 1989, p. 96).

The local option tends to conflict with professional education, mainly because the latter does not address the immediate problems that the local option is confronting. As Freire (1970, p. 84) states, "one cannot expect positive results from an educational or political action program which fails to respect the particular view of the world held by the people." That is to say, local options are much clearer than the state models about the contradictions of an educational system that considers itself democratic but does not promote real participation by all groups. On this basis, we can explain how programs such as Universidad Popular in Chicago started when the educational system was confronted through critical analysis of the reality of those participating in the program. As described by Heany (1989, p. 3), "housed in a narrow storefront on Belmont Avenue, sandwiched between a taco restaurant and a health clinic, was one of the most successful adult education centers. It survived nine tumultuous years of struggle between the Latino community and the City Colleges of Chicago. The issue over which they fought was community control. Several organizations contributed to its beginning. An educational philosophy and purpose began to emerge from a variety of adult education classes long before the concept of a community center had developed." Education, to be effective, must be linked to the community's problems as well as incorporate the community resources. It is evident that in this case local control was an extremely important issue. Two organizations, the Latin American Coalition of Lakeview, a grass-roots organization, and the Jane Adams Hull House Center, "wanted to create an adult education center under local control, responsive to neighborhood issues and concerns" (Heany, 1989, p. 3).

Organization. There are many activities and programs of popular education that are created from and within organizations that serve a variety of social needs. One negative aspect of many of these programs is that those involved in developing the plans or assisting program implementation may not acknowledge the capacity of people organizing and developing their own agendas. Organizing the curricula of programs for them, without their input, does not represent the legitimate interest of the community. Such exclusion in turn promotes attitudes of individualism, passiveness, dependency, and competitiveness. Therefore, the popular educational process should be pursued from the standpoint of the reality of the groups or organizations that will be served by the programs. The educational process as seen from the perspective of a base organization has specific characteristics: It is democratic, critical, creative, participatory, permanent, autonomous, and integrated (Ghiso, 1989). Essentially, this educational practice is oriented toward community participation in order to recognize and maintain the diverse identities, experiences, and needs of local groups.

Participation. Participation has become an important issue not only in education but also in other areas of society. The problem is that the concept of participation depends on the political-ideological conception of the person promoting a program. Therefore, what is important is not participation per se but rather the content and scope of the program where the participation takes place, with its political and ideological implications (Ghiso, 1989, p. 116). In order to encourage participation, the decision-making process should not be authoritarian in character but instead democratic. In other words, participation in the educational process serves to develop solidarity, pluralism, and respect for diverse social realities, and even to promote change.

As we can see with many projects of popular education, organization, level of participation, and clarity of goals vary a great deal from program to program. In this respect the accounts of Universidad Popular in Chicago show some of the problems enumerated earlier: "Hull House contributed financially to the project. During the first two years, the center staff participated in weekly staff meetings at Hull House, learning from their considerable experience in building programs with neighborhood resources. . . . [But Hull House also] imposed a service orientation which emphasized symptoms, not the political and the economic roots of poverty, discrimination, and unemployment" (Heany, 1989, p. 3). Since Universidad Popular was organized around three entities—the Latin American Coalition, Hull House, and the Center for Continuing Education at Loop College, one of the city colleges of Chicago—in order to draft a proposal for funding, all of them contributed to the new organization and represented their respective points of view. Accordingly, Hull House contributed financially, the Center for Continuing Education contributed the philosophy of theory and action espoused by Paulo Freire, and the Latin American Coalition provided knowledge and information about the community as an instrument of social change so that learning could lead to effective action (Heany, 1989). In this case it seems that the organizational and participatory component was not as clear as it could have been. As Heany (1989, p. 3) has noted, "the Coalition urged its own agenda: the development of a multiservice center, only one component of which was adult education. This agenda . . . diverted staff and board attention from developing a curriculum responsive to the community during the critical early years of the project."

The Universidad Popular program is probably one of the few programs that has attempted to reconcile existing popular knowledge and solutions drawn from community initiatives with the arid conceptualizations of higher education. "Thus the college and the community could enter into a collegial relationship with astonishing results not previously achieved by either college or community alone" (Heany, 1989, p. 4). In this case the minority community was conscious of its own dependency, unemployment, and language barriers and was able to have a vision of its own reality. However, programs such as Universidad Popular are seen by many critics as "marginal," which translates to little or no political participation by the local communities and little voice in the formulation of solutions to their own problems. Political participation by many is reduced to undemocratic political manipulation by a few. Programs such as Universidad Popular represent the "dynamics in the contested terrain of culture in the relationship between the hegemonic and subordinated classes. The struggle was against a college which was at the end a fiscal agency accountable for the operations of programs" (Heany, 1989, p. 4). Universidad Popular, despite all the problems it endured, was able to offer "traditional ESL and GED classes. Workshops were organized around neighborhood issues: gentrification, budget reductions affecting bilingual education, discrimination in employment, civil rights, women's rights, and health care issues. By 1974 enrollment was up to 370 students" (Heany, 1989, p. 6).

Through the years Universidad Popular survived difficult times in a battle for local control and against the bureaucratic and official educational establishment. The development and process of the program provided a "critical analysis of the role of schooling" (Heany, 1989, p. 11). What has been accomplished up to the present seems a historical landmark of many popular education programs. As alluded to earlier, in programs that are labeled popular education some characteristics are essential. The need for solidarity is manifested in common purposes, which lead to creativity in finding solutions and linking those solutions to political life. We need to be clear in our purpose and remain open to criticism.

The experiences and success of Universidad Popular have been noticed by community leaders. In fall 1988 a group of community organization leaders in the Pilsen neighborhood of Chicago met with the faculty of adult education at Northern Illinois University to discuss the possibility of offering a master's degree in adult education, with an emphasis on community action. The community's main concern was the need to develop a strong core of leaders who, having the experience of working everyday in the field, would be able to acquire a university degree in a participatory, democratic environment. A program was established, designed to prepare individuals as urban educational leaders capable of addressing the current and future issues related to adult learning, for example, political trends, funding, urban policy, and adult literacy. By the end of the program it is expected that the participants will be able to understand the decision-making and funding processes of corporate and educational programs, and of community and proprietary agencies. They will also be able to articulate a philosophy and vision of community education, while understanding adult development, adult learning, and patterns of participation in educational settings.

At present the program has more than twenty participants, most of whom are either program directors for community agencies or workers within those agencies. As field workers, all of them are in direct and regular contact with the Pilsen community. Classes conducted under the auspices of Northern Illinois University are held during weekends through a program already designed by the faculty of adult education. Classes are not held on campus but rather in the Pilsen community, using the facilities of a community agency. The program entails thirty hours of course work, including six credit hours for internship experience and six for the project requirement. Classes include discussion of the work experiences of the students and of how to strengthen the participation of residents in order to become more effective in their community. The students are mostly from the minority community in Chicago and their work is mostly conducted in that community. In order to obtain the degree, a final project has been included as an integral part of the whole process. This project is intended to provide the students with an opportunity to engage in guided investigation in topics of their choice. The guidelines for each project are developed in consultation between the adviser and the student in order to facilitate its conclusion.

This master's degree program is an attempt to engage the participants in alternative forms of education. Even if the program is not considered popular education, many of the definitive elements are present, such as the idea of change and the ability of participants to effect change.

Interpretation and Conclusion

There is general consensus that in adult education certain factors are necessary in order to have successful programs, especially factors pertaining to the social contexts in which participants work. A program's success depends to a great extent on its flexibility and the applicability of its content to the cultural, political, and socioeconomic reality of the participants. Although most of us may agree that attention to these conceptual categories is important, incorporating multiple visions of social reality and of educational practice into a coherent program is difficult. I agree with Ghiso's (1989, p. 112) comment that some of the problems in the current practice of popular education are owing to the fact that "as educators we see and characterize reality from a general and schematic point of view." This in turn brings negative consequences that affect the educational program as a real catalyst for social change. The reason for working on generalities springs from the following six points:

1. Popular educators lack precise knowledge. No diagnoses of problems are performed, little information is requested, and only the general characteristics of the reality of participants are known.
2. There is little clarity in naming the reality, and in characterizing concrete situations for the construction of a new social order. As a result there is no critical context to sustain the educational project.
3. There is no linkage between what popular educators do and their orientation and knowledge about community groups.

4. Program planners tend to respond mostly to specific concerns but do not always think carefully about situations within the community.

5. Popular educators need formation (training) that shows the value of characterizing reality and analyzing critically visions of social change.

6. Popular education represents an alternative for adult educators who are genuinely interested in the participation of those segments of society who defy the rules imposed on them and seek truly to remake the world. Communication and collaboration among those groups are essential in order to create an environment that allows different cultures to be represented in a truly equal way.

References

Adams, F., and Horton, M. *Unearthing Seeds of Fire: The Idea of Highlander.* Winston-Salem, N.C.: Blair, 1975.

Freire, P. *Pedagogy of the Oppressed.* New York: Seabury Press, 1970.

Ghiso, A. "Educación de adultos, un camino por hacer" [Adult education: A road for doing]. In *La formación metodologica de los educadores populares* [Methodological formation of popular educators]. Documento del Colectivo de Apoyo Metodologico del Consejo de Educación de Adultos de America Latina (CEEAL). Santiago, Chile: CEEAL, 1989.

Heany, T. *Struggling to Be Free.* De Kalb: Lindeman Center, Northern Illinois University, 1989.

Mejia, M. P. "Formación de educadores populares: búsqueda y reto de una practica alternativa" [Formation of popular educators: The search for and challenge of a practical alternative]. In *La formación metodologica de los educadores populares* [Methodological formation of popular educators]. Documento del Colectivo de Apoyo Metodologico del Consejo de Educación de Adultos de America Latina (CEEAL). Santiago, Chile: CEEAL, 1989.

Ormeno, O. "Producción de conocimientos y experiencias en la formación de educadores de adultos" [Production of knowledge and experience in the formation of educators of adults]. In *La formación metodologica de los educadores populares* [Methodological formation of popular educators]. Documento del Colectivo de Apoyo Metodologico del Consejo de Educación de Adultos de America Latina (CEEAL). Santiago, Chile: CEEAL, 1989.

Pollard, H. *Pioneers of Popular Education.* Cambridge, Mass.: Harvard University Press, 1957.

Prajuli, P. "Grassroot Movements, Development Discourse, and Popular Education." *Convergence,* 1988, 23 (3).

Vio Grossi, F. *Educación popular y politica en America Latina* [Popular and political education in Latin America]. Serie Educación Popular y Democracia, no. 1. Santiago, Chile: Consejo de Educación de Adultos de America Latina (CEEAL), 1989.

Jorge Jeria is assistant professor of adult education at Northern Illinois University, De Kalb, and a faculty associate of the Northern Illinois Consortium for Research.

CONCLUSION

A review of the chapters presented here reveals certain themes regarding existing barriers to minority participation in adult and continuing education, as well as factors associated with programs effectively serving culturally diverse adults. This concluding chapter presents both an analysis of these themes and a discussion of implications for practice.

Barriers to Participation

The themes in this volume regarding barriers to participation take on a more sociological or sociocultural tone than typically found in models of adult education participation, such as those of Cross (1981) or Darkenwald and Merriam (1982). While sociological dimensions are included in the models presented by Miller (1967) and Rubenson (cited in Cross, 1981), the authors included here have given more attention to social-structural barriers and conflicts involving culturally based values than found in those models. Among social-structural dimensions, Martin (Chapter Two) discusses the structural barriers that have become prominent in the inner-city as a result of a changing economy and shifting political priorities. These barriers include unemployment, lack of preparation for jobs in the new economic structure, and physical isolation from the mainstream. Data presented by Ross-Gordon (Chapter One) on the availability of employer-provided education to minorities also suggest that unequal access to this growing segment of adult education activity may be a structural barrier. Martin, Nardine (Chapter Six), and Jeria (Chapter Eight) also speak in various ways of the disempowerment or disenfranchisement experienced by minority adults as they attempt either to interact with the educational system (Nardine and Jeria) or to have a role in democratic political processes (Martin and Jeria).

Conflicts between the culture of the educational institution and the culture of the prospective student also surface as barriers in the discussions of several of the authors. Podeschi (Chapter Five) speaks of the tension ever present between pluralism and assimilation at a general societal level. This tension in the larger society also appears to affect prospective adult students who may or may not be willing to risk possible alienation from their cultural bonds as they adopt the behaviors, language, and values of the larger society. Several authors draw on the work of Ogbu (1978, 1987, 1990) in describing this tension, as evidenced in the behavior of students and manifest in what Ogbu calls cultural inversion. Thus, students may appear to actively oppose the norms of the educational institution as they seek to assert their own cultural identities. This behavior seems consistent with resistance theory (Giroux, 1983), presented here as a possible explanation for nonparticipation by Ross-Gordon. Martin refers to fictive kinship (Fordham, 1988) and primary discourse (Gee, 1989) as additional concepts explaining the tendency for some minority students to behave in a way that supports their ties to their respective primary cultural groups rather than to the larger, dominant society. Such patterns may explain the reluctance of many minority adults to involve themselves with formal adult education programs that are associated with dominant social institutions, or their failure to persist in programs that emphasize dominant cultural values and behaviors.

Cultural influences on preferred learning processes or styles also are referred to by Briscoe (Chapter Seven) and Podeschi. Both speak of the predominant emphasis on individualism in contemporary American society, contrasting it with values for greater interdependence seen in earlier American society and in cultures from which many minority group adults originate. Briscoe speaks of collaboration and interdependence as hallmarks of community education, offering minority adults a level of cooperative involvement not easily available in other structures. Podeschi notes that interdependent and holistic learning was preferred by the Hmong refugees in the program he describes, over the more individualistic and analytical learning-instructional models characteristic of many adult education programs. In trying to assign the Hmong English as a Second Language (ESL) program to one of two major literacy program models, he observes that the literacy model developed by the Hmong fits neither an individualistic basic-skills model nor a social action empowerment model. Instead, it incorporates the skills emphasis of the first model with the community-based orientation of the second. The interest of the Hmong in interdependent, socially connected learning was honored in this unique variation. Thus, this program escapes the barrier that both Martin and Podeschi decry, that of the culturally insensitive adult education program.

Factors Associated with Effective Programs

As might be anticipated, all of the principles suggested here as criteria for "model" programs were also confirmed as elements of the effective programs mentioned in the chapters. In addition, several new themes emerged as characteristic of the effective programs described.

Original Program Criteria. The following elements of effective programs were originally listed as criteria for selecting programs for discussion:

1. *Preserving cultural distinctness of groups in programming.* This element seemed especially salient in the descriptions by Podeschi and Moe (Chapter Three) of programs offered to the Hmong refugees and Navajo Indians. These descriptions confirm that even programs designed for other minorities

may be inadequate in preserving or reaffirming the distinct cultural legacy and learning preferences of a specific group. ESL programs developed for Hispanics in Milwaukee did not meet the needs of the Hmong as effectively as the literacy program designed by and for the Hmong themselves.

2. *Accommodating preferred learning strategies or learning environments.* The importance of this element was made most explicit in the program description by Podeschi and in the narratives of Briscoe and Martin. Preferences for more interdependent and holistic teaching-learning models by some minority learners is in nearly direct conflict with the individualistic and analytical learning styles emphasized in many adult education programs. This conflict calls into question even the emphasis on self-directed learning, which is a fundamental tenet of much of contemporary North American adult education, if in fact certain minority groups reject the individual achievement assumptions on which this tenet rests. Preferences for certain learning environments also appear to be either explicit or implicit in the discussions of model programs by Martin, Nardine, and Podeschi. All three describe programs that offer sufficient informality and flexibility within an overall guiding structure. Podeschi speaks as well of the need for the Hmong to look up to their instructors with a certain degree of respect, while still viewing them as approachable.

3. *Utilizing existing social networks.* The value of incorporating such networks in recruitment and program planning comes through most clearly in the chapters by Briscoe and Podeschi. It seems evident from their discussions that effective adult education programs can also help bring people into new and expanded social networks that include others who are culturally similar and share an interest in gaining knowledge or skills.

4. *Empowering learners to change their lives and communities.* The chapters by Briscoe on community education and by Jeria on popular education clearly exemplify an emphasis on both individual- and community-level empowerment. Additionally, Nardine's discussion of parental involvement in the education of their children, Martin's discussion of literacy education, and Moe's discussion of higher education give considerable emphasis to the importance of learner empowerment.

5. *Preparing learners for life and career development beyond short-term occupational goals.* Development of basic skills as a foundation for future learning is emphasized in the programs described by Martin and Podeschi, while skill development at a higher level is provided by the Minority Continuing Education Opportunity Program (MCEOP) described by Moe. Similarly, the learners in the Youth Action Program described by Briscoe learn occupational and basic skills that will assist them beyond their participation in the program.

6. *Supporting minority families in their pursuit of learning goals.* Nardine's chapter on parental involvement focuses on an obvious example of these

principles. The program he describes supports the philosophy of a "direct child-indirect parent" approach to family learning, involving, first, school children and then their parents in the acquisition of computer skills.

7. *Reaching out to the most disenfranchised.* Clearly, this is a focus in the programs described by Briscoe for young adults who are often characterized as "at risk." Her description of a program reaching back into the high school has been included in this volume on adult and continuing education because such initiatives seem vital to efforts to reach young people, often functioning socially as adults outside the high school, before they have disengaged from education. Nardine's chapter looks at efforts to reach disenfranchised parents and increase their involvement with the schools. This form of intervention also is likely to have long-term, indirect consequences on enrollment by minorities in adult education, as family support for education of their children becomes stronger and more concrete when family-school interactions are enhanced. Thus, school non-completion may become less of a likelihood for children in such families.

8. *Utilizing creative financing of adult learning opportunities.* MCEOP, described by Moe, clearly illustrates this principle, as local businesses subsidize the enrollment of their employees in MCEOP at Ohio State University through a tuition-recycling strategy. Other programs, mentioned by Briscoe, Jeria, and Podeschi have made creative use of private and public sources of funding, often in combination, to support educational activities sponsored for minority adults or to sponsor support services such as day care.

9. *Sponsoring activities that increase the level of intercultural sensitivity of staff.* This element is mentioned only in Chapter Four by Martin and Ross-Gordon on learning in the workplace. This focus either has not reached other segments of adult education or was simply not mentioned in a significant fashion in the program descriptions presented by the chapter authors.

Emergent Themes. The following elements of effective programs were not originally listed as criteria for selecting programs for discussion:

1. *Community-based.* The location of programs in the local community appears to be a salient feature for programs described by Briscoe, Jeria, and Podeschi. Ease of access, linkages to social networks, and interest in locally relevant issues all appear to be features associated with the success of community-based programs.

2. *Relationships between the day-to-day world and formal instruction.* Noted by Podeschi in his description of the Hmong literacy program, this program characteristic may to some extent be linked to the community-based context of some adult education programs. As a program dimension, however, it can also be incorporated into programs offered by institutional sponsors who are not community-based. The key to this dimension seems to be instructional planning that involves the student or, at a minimum, recognizes the critical learning needs in the community of learners.

3. *Teaching their own.* Podeschi suggests there is a unique advantage in

the Hmong literacy program that he describes because the instructors come from and thus understand the cultural background of the students. Earlier work by Darkenwald (1975) suggested that Black adult basic education (ABE) teachers were more successful than White teachers in retaining ABE students in large cities, where a large proportion of ABE students were Black. Different emphases on nontraditional curricula, with Black teachers more likely to focus on the day-to-day learning needs mentioned directly above, accounted in part for the differences between Black and White teachers holding power, but significant differences remained even after accounting for instructional empha-sis. Darkenwald posited that either of two factors could account for these differences. Improved communication based on shared language patterns and shared knowledge provided one possible explanation, while a greater degree of comfort of students with teachers similar in cultural background provided an alternative explanation. Noting that White teachers who emphasized non-traditional curricula were more successful than Whites who did not, he sug-gested this teaching strategy at least signified their recognition of the life situations of their students, and perhaps also their greater cultural under-standing of the students. While interpretation of the findings of this study is problematic because of Darkenwald's failure to verify each student's race, the data nonetheless suggest the need for further investigation of the impact of shared cultural backgrounds, or, at a minimum, cultural sensitivity, as a vari-able affecting minority student retention and learning.

4. *Institutional collaboration.* This emerged as an important element in several of the programs described. Combinations of collaborators included corporate and university partners (MCEOP); law enforcement agencies, banks, religious institutions, and a federal job program (Youth Action Pro-gram); and a settlement house, university continuing education program, and Latin American volunteer association (Universidad Popular). Such link-ages require the creative efforts of key individuals who have a vision of how organizations with such diverse purposes can work together. As Jeria points out, such collaboration is inherently complex.

5. *Taking advantage of technology.* Computers were used as an instruc-tional aide in programs described by Martin and Nardine. Distance edu-cation-delivery modes were supported as a viable way to provide educa-tion on the Navajo reservation, as mentioned by Moe. As various forms of distance education and computer-assisted instruction become increas-ingly utilized within adult and continuing education, it is essential that minority adults have equal access to the advantages of the latest educa-tional technologies.

What Practitioners Can Do

Those of us who seek to broaden the access of culturally diverse adults to adult education programs will need to play a proactive role in altering traditions within our own institutional frameworks of adults and continuing education.

1. Improve our knowledge and understanding of other cultural groups, particularly those within our respective service areas. This can be done in a variety of formal and informal ways. A first step may be simply getting to know on a personal level students or professional colleagues who represent a given cultural background. Other self-education options vary along a range of formality, from viewing relevant television programming or reading novels written by members of the culture, to attending workshops on cultural diversity.

2. Incorporate as principles of good practice those program criteria reviewed in this chapter, since they can be made applicable to individual programs and professional practices.

3. Network or collaborate with others who have experienced success in working with diverse populations and seek to build on their successes within our own programs. Many successful programs can be found in our own communities.

4. Identify institutions that by the nature of their specialized missions are invaluable as resources in serving culturally diverse adults, for example, Black colleges, Native American community colleges, and research and development centers on minority education.

5. Work within our respective institutions to create climates that are more responsive to the needs of culturally diverse groups.

6. Work within our professional organizations to increase conference programming, publications, and political advocacy that address and promote the needs of culturally diverse adults.

7. In the realm of civic activities, speak and act in a fashion that is consistent with our enlightened beliefs on the importance of broadening access to effective adult and continuing education programs. Thus, we can carry on in the tradition of Alain Locke, an African-American famous for his contributions to the Harlem renaissance but less well known as a founding member of the American Association for Adult Education (AAAE). In his presidential address to AAAE, Locke (1947, p. 104) proclaimed as an essential aim of adult education "the democratic widening of all sorts of education opportunities and experiences for more and more people over greater areas not only of knowledge and skills but for effective self-knowledge and understanding."

Jovita M. Ross-Gordon
Larry G. Martin
Diane Buck Briscoe
Editors

References

Cross, K. P. *Adults as Learners: Increasing Participation and Facilitating Learning.* San Francisco: Jossey-Bass, 1981.

Darkenwald, G. G. "Some Effects of the 'Obvious Variable': Teacher's Race and Holding Power with Black Adult Students." *Sociology of Education*, 1975, 48 (2), 420–431.

Darkenwald, G. G., and Merriam, S. B. *Adult Education: Foundations of Practice.* New York: Harper & Row, 1982.

Fordham, S. "Racelessness as a Factor in Black Students' School Success: Pragmatic Strategy or Pyrrhic Victory?" *Harvard Educational Review*, 1988, 58 (1), 54–84.

Gee, P. J. "Literacy, Discourse, and Linguistics: Introduction." *Journal of Education*, 1989, 171 (1), 5–17.

Giroux, H. "Theories of Reproduction: Resistance in the New Sociology of Education: A Critical Analysis." *Harvard Educational Review*, 1983, 53 (3), 257–293.

Locke, A. "Education for Adulthood." *Adult Education Journal*, 1947, 6, 104–111.

Miller, H. L. *Participation of Adults in Education: A Forcefield Analysis.* Boston: Center for the Study of Liberal Education for Adults, Boston University, 1967.

Ogbu, J. U. *Minority Education and Caste: The American System in Cross-Cultural Perspective.* Orlando, Fla.: Academic Press, 1978.

Ogbu, J. U. "Variability in Minority Responses to Schooling: Nonimmigrants Versus Immigrants." In G. Spindler and L. Spindler (eds.), *Interpretive Ethnography of Education: At Home and Abroad.* Hillsdale, N.J.: Erlbaum, 1987.

Ogbu, J. U. "Minority Status and Literacy in Comparative Perspective." *Daedalus*, 1990, 119 (2), 141–168.

Jovita M. Ross-Gordon is assistant professor of adult education at The Pennsylvania State University, University Park.

Larry G. Martin is associate professor of adult and continuing education at the University of Wisconsin, Milwaukee.

Diane Buck Briscoe is assistant professor of adult education at the University of South Florida, Tampa.

INDEX

Abonyi, M. H., 13, 14
Adams, F., 94, 100
Adcock, B., 83, 90
Adult basic education (ABE), 2, 105
Adult education: domains of, 2-3; participation levels for, 6-9; suggestions for improving, 105-106
Adult literacy programs: culturally insensitive, 25-26; history of, 19-20; minority participation in, 20-22; model for, 26-28. *See also* Literacy education
African-Americans, 18, 33, 57, 63, 82, 83; adult literacy of, 19-22; participation by, 7-8; participation barriers for, 23, 24-25; in population, 5-6; in work force, 46, 47, 49, 50-51. *See also* Blacks
Allen, G., 84, 85, 86, 90
American Indians, 18, 22, 57; education demographics for, 35-36; Navajo Community College for, 40; Smithsonian Museum of, 40-41. *See also* Native Americans
Apple, M., 12, 13
Apps, J., 7, 13
Apps, J. W., 37, 42
Arbeiter, S., 34, 42
Argyris, C., 50, 51, 53
Asians, 18, 57; adult literacy of, 20, 22; participation by, 8; in population, 6. *See also* Hmong
Atwell, R. H., 34, 42

Baba, M. L., 13, 14
Baker, P. C., 31
Bastiani, J., 84, 85, 86, 90
Becher, R. M., 75, 79
Beder, H., 85, 90
Belkin, L., 87, 88, 90
Berg, I., 9, 15
Bernick, M., 26, 28
Berrol, S., 56, 64
Bialo, E. R., 74, 79
Blacks, 105; education demographics for, 35-37; participation by, 6-8; and popular education, 94. *See also* African-Americans
Bok, D., 31, 42

Briscoe, D. B., 2, 3, 34, 42, 63, 64, 81, 85, 90, 91, 102, 103, 104, 106, 107
Bronfenbrenner, U., 70, 71, 79
Brookfield, S. D., 37, 42
Bryant, L., 84, 90

Campbell, C. M., 86, 90
Carnevale, A. P., 48, 49, 53
Carter, D., 8, 15
Cartwright, M., 3, 5, 14
Cavazos, L. F., 67, 79
Chain of Response model, 10
Chase, N. D., 52, 54
Chatham, R. L., 13, 14
Clark, D., 83, 90
Cochran, M., 71, 72, 75, 79
Cohen, D. K., 70, 79
Colburn, J., 83, 90
Coleman, J., 70, 79
College Entrance Examination Board, 34, 42
Comer, J. P., 73, 79
Community education, 2-3, 84-85, 89-90; history of, 81-84; models of, 85-86; programs for, 86-89
Computer education, minority parental involvement in, 74-79
Copeland, L., 45, 54
Cremin, L. A., 31, 42
Cross, K. P., 9, 10, 11, 14, 89, 90, 101, 107
Cultural diversity, 5-6; and adult education participation, 6-13; and democracy, 39-41; demographics of, 34-37; and education, 31-32, 37-39; program types for, 52-53; of work force, 46-48; in workplace, 45-46, 53; workplace management of, 48-52. *See also* Minorities
Cultural inversion, 22, 101
Cultural pluralism, 31-32
Culture: and literacy education, 56-58; organizational, 49-51
Cunningham, P., 13, 14

Darkenwald, G., 22, 29
Darkenwald, G. G., 7, 12, 14, 37, 42, 101, 105, 107

109

ORDERING INFORMATION

NEW DIRECTIONS FOR ADULT AND CONTINUING EDUCATION is a series of paperback books that explores issues of common interest to instructors, administrators, counselors, and policy makers in a broad range of adult and continuing education settings—such as colleges and universities, extension programs, businesses, the military, prisons, libraries, and museums. Books in the series are published quarterly in Fall, Winter, Spring, and Summer and are available for purchase by subscription as well as by single copy.

SUBSCRIPTIONS for 1990 cost $42.00 for individuals (a savings of 20 percent over single-copy prices) and $56.00 for institutions, agencies, and libraries. Please do not send institutional checks for personal subscriptions. Standing orders are accepted.

SINGLE COPIES cost $12.95 when payment accompanies order. (California, New Jersey, New York, and Washington, D.C., residents please include appropriate sales tax.) Billed orders will be charged postage and handling.

DISCOUNTS FOR QUANTITY ORDERS are available. Please write to the address below for information.

ALL ORDERS must include either the name of an individual or an official purchase order number. Please submit your order as follows:
Subscriptions: specify series and year subscription is to begin
Single copies: include individual title code (such as CE1)

MAIL ALL ORDERS TO:
Jossey-Bass Inc., Publishers
350 Sansome Street
San Francisco, California 94104

FOR SALES OUTSIDE OF THE UNITED STATES CONTACT:
Maxwell Macmillan International Publishing Group
866 Third Avenue
New York, New York 10022

OTHER TITLES AVAILABLE IN THE
NEW DIRECTIONS FOR ADULT AND CONTINUING EDUCATION SERIES
Ralph G. Brockett, Editor-in-Chief
Alan B. Knox, Consulting Editor

U.S. Postal Service

STATEMENT OF OWNERSHIP, MANAGEMENT AND CIRCULATION
Required by 39 U.S.C. 3685

1A. Title of Publication	1B. PUBLICATION NO.	2. Date of Filing
New Directions for Adult and Continuing Education	4 9 3 - 5 3 0	9/18/90

3. Frequency of Issue	3A. No. of Issues Published Annually	3B. Annual Subscription Price
Quarterly	Four (4)	$45 (individual) $60 (institutional)

4. Complete Mailing Address of Known Office of Publication (Street, City, County, State and ZIP+4 Code) (Not printers)

350 Sansome Street, San Francisco, CA 94104-1310

5. Complete Mailing Address of the Headquarters of General Business Offices of the Publisher (Not printer)

(above address)

6. Full Names and Complete Mailing Address of Publisher, Editor, and Managing Editor (This item MUST NOT be blank)

Publisher (Name and Complete Mailing Address)

Jossey-Bass Inc., Publishers (above address)

Editor (Name and Complete Mailing Address)

Ralph G. Brockett, University of Tennessee, 402 Claxton Addition,
Knoxville, TN 37996-3400

Managing Editor (Name and Complete Mailing Address)

Steven Piersanti, President, Jossey-Bass Inc., Publishers (above address)

7. Owner (If owned by a corporation, its name and address must be stated and also immediately thereunder the names and addresses of stockholders owning or holding 1 percent or more of total amount of stock. If not owned by a corporation, the names and addresses of the individual owners must be given. If owned by a partnership or other unincorporated firm, its name and address, as well as that of each individual must be given. If the publication is published by a nonprofit organization, its name and address must be stated.) (Item must be completed.)

Full Name	Complete Mailing Address
Maxwell Communications Corp., plc	Headington Hill Hall Oxford OX30BW U.K.

8. Known Bondholders, Mortgagees, and Other Security Holders Owning or Holding 1 Percent or More of Total Amount of Bonds, Mortgages or Other Securities (If there are none, so state)

Full Name	Complete Mailing Address
same as above	same as above

9. For Completion by Nonprofit Organizations Authorized To Mail at Special Rates (DMM Section 423.12 only)
The purpose, function, and nonprofit status of this organization and the exempt status for Federal income tax purposes (Check one)

☐ (1) Has Not Changed During Preceding 12 Months ☐ (2) Has Changed During Preceding 12 Months (If changed, publisher must submit explanation of change with this statement.)

10.	Extent and Nature of Circulation (See instructions on reverse side)	Average No. Copies Each Issue During Preceding 12 Months	Actual No. Copies of Single Issue Published Nearest to Filing Date
A.	Total No. Copies (Net Press Run)	1600	1719
B.	Paid and/or Requested Circulation 1. Sales through dealers and carriers, street vendors and counter sales	375	298
	2. Mail Subscription (Paid and/or requested)	698	420
C.	Total Paid and/or Requested Circulation (Sum of 10B1 and 10B2)	1073	718
D.	Free Distribution by Mail, Carrier or Other Means Samples, Complimentary, and Other Free Copies	84	80
E.	Total Distribution (Sum of C and D)	1157	798
F.	Copies Not Distributed 1. Office use, left over, unaccounted, spoiled after printing	443	921
	2. Return from News Agents	0	0
G.	TOTAL (Sum of E, F1 and 2—should equal net press run shown in A)	1600	1719

11. I certify that the statements made by me above are correct and complete	Signature and Title of Editor, Publisher, Business Manager, or Owner  Larry Ishii Vice-President

PS Form **3526**, Feb. 1989   (See instructions on reverse)